What About?
Jack Russell Terriers

Audrey Pavia

HOWELL
BOOK
HOUSE

Howell Book House
Published by Wiley Publishing, Inc., Indianapolis, IN

For general information on our other products and services or to obtain technical support please contact our Customer Care Department within the U.S. at 800-762-2974, outside the U.S. at 317-572-3993 or fax 317-572-4002.

Wiley also publishes its books in a variety of electronic formats. Some content that appears in print may not be available in electronic books.

Library of Congress Control Number: 2003105645

ISBN: 0-764-54089-0

Manufactured in the United States of America

10 9 8 7 6 5 4 3 2 1

All photos © Kent and Donna Dannen
Book production by Wiley Publishing, Inc. Composition Services

Contents

How Can I Learn More?   142

Index   148

1

What Exactly Is a Jack Russell Terrier?

 What exactly is a Jack Russell Terrier? • Why are Jack Russell Terriers such good hunters? • Why are Jack Russell Terriers so popular? • How long do Jack Russells live? • How active are Jack Russell Terriers? • What are 10 good reasons to want a Jack Russell Terrier? • Do Jack Russell Terriers make good apartment dogs? • What are 10 bad reasons to want a Jack Russell Terrier? • What are the top 10 reasons people give up their Jack Russell Terriers? • Do Jack Russell Terriers bark very much? • Are Jack Russells hard to house-train? • How big do Jack Russells get? • Do Jack Russells shed? • Are Jack Russells friendly with strangers?

What exactly is a Jack Russell Terrier?

He's a feisty, incredibly active little terrier who, despite weighing only from 8 to 15 pounds, thinks he is a large dog. Jack Russells vary in height, and can be anywhere from 10 inches at the top of the shoulder to 15 inches. They are usually white with black or tan markings, or a combination of both. They come in two different coat types: smooth or broken-haired.

What else are Jack Russell Terriers called?

The American Kennel Club uses the term Parson Russell Terriers, as they do in England. In this book, we will call them the name they have long been known by in this country, which is Jack Russell Terriers, or the shortened version, Jacks.

What are Jack Russell Terriers used for? Why?

Jack Russells are tough, outdoor dogs used for hunting small animals, for competitive canine sports and for companionship. They have a very powerful hunting instinct that has been bred into them for centuries, making them among the best hunting dogs around.

Jack Russell Terriers were originally bred to "go to ground"—that is, to follow prey underneath the ground. When a fox, rabbit or other rodent tries to escape by running into its underground burrow, the Jack follows the animal into the burrow. The Jack then catches the animal on the run or after it has been cornered, and kills the prey. The prey sometimes fights back, which means the Jack Russell has to be a brave, tough little dog to stand up to this defensive attack.

Today, people are able to use the Jack Russell's talents in a variety of ways. The dogs compete successfully in terrier hunting competitions (called earthdog trials), do well in sports that require running and jumping and are great for keeping farms and ranches free from rodents.

Why are Jack Russell Terriers such good hunters?

They are tenacious, fearless and relentless. Jack Russells have been known to follow prey for miles and miles without giving up. Once they catch their prey, they usually kill it. Their prey can include anything from a wild rabbit to the neighbor's cat.

In the 1800s and early 1900s, Jack Russells were used during foxhunts to pursue the fox once the animal had retreated into its burrow. While the foxhounds "gave voice"—that is, bayed loudly so the hunter would know where the fox had hidden, the Jack Russell went into the fox's burrow and sought to chase the fox out so the hunter could kill it. Since a fox is about the same size as a Jack Russell, it took a tough little terrier to tackle this job underground.

Jack Russells use almost all their senses when hunting. They listen to hear their prey and use their noses to follow its scent. They are quick to catch sight of an animal on the run with their good vision. They also use their intelligence to outsmart animals who are trying to escape by running through a series of underground burrows.

How did Jack Russells get this strong hunting instinct?

Farmers living in England have bred them for hundreds of years to be aggressive hunters. Animals such as rats, mice and gophers plagued farmers by eating their crops and making nests and burrows on their property. These farmers needed a dog who could work on its own to hunt down these rodents and kill them.

Jack Russells were also used by foxhunters to help in the hunt, and were bred in part for this use. Since the fox is an animal who fights back when cornered by a dog, foxhunters needed a dog with incredible spunk and courage for this kind of hunting.

What do Jack Russells do when they are hunting?

If their prey is above ground, they will chase their prey until they catch it, and will kill it if they can. They will run the prey down until the animal is too exhausted to run any further. Or they will corner the prey until they are able to grasp it in their jaws or underneath their paws. If the animal goes into an underground burrow, the Jack Russell will follow, racing through the animal's burrows until he corners the creature. If the burrow is too small for the Jack to fit, the dog will dig his way into the burrow until he unearths the prey.

Rodents hiding in haystacks, between walls or underneath woodpiles are not safe from this breed. Jack Russells will dig or chew their way through any kind of barrier to get access to their prey. In fact, one Jack in California tore a huge hole in his owner's living room wall because he heard a mouse squeaking inside.

Why are Jack Russell Terriers so popular?

Jack Russells have an endearing appearance. They have bright eyes, neat little ears and an inquisitive look. Many people have seen dogs like Eddie on the NBC sitcom *Frasier* and the dog who plays Wishbone on the PBS special of the same name, and think Jacks are cute and mellow like those TV dogs. What they don't realize is that the average Jack Russell is nothing like Eddie or Wishbone. Many Jack Russell Terriers end up abandoned by their owners because most people can't handle these complex dogs.

People who enjoy living with this breed appreciate their dog's difficult personality, and even boast about it. They think it's fun to have a busy, mischievous dog who always gets into trouble around every turn.

How are Jack Russells not like Eddie or Wishbone?

The Jack Russells you see on TV are acting in more ways than one. They are not just pretending to be Eddie or Wishbone, they are pretending to be nice, well-behaved dogs. You could even say they are acting like a breed other than a Jack Russell Terrier!

The Jacks who play Eddie and Wishbone have undergone thousands of hours of specialized training to get them to behave the way they do on TV, and put on a ruse of being mellow and easygoing. In real life, these same dogs are typical Jack Russell Terriers: they are extremely active and often get into trouble. In fact, trainers who work with movie animals look for dogs with a lot of energy and drive for this kind of work. That same energy and drive that makes them great movie dogs can make them terrible pets who will drive their owners nuts.

The good behavior of Jack Russell Terrier actors is usually limited to the short periods of time they are required to be in front of the camera. In fact, before he was finally adopted by his current trainer, one of the Jack Russell Terriers who played Eddie on *Frasier* was abandoned twice by pet owners who couldn't deal with him.

How long do Jack Russells live?

Jack Russells often live to be 16 years old, and stay active right up until the end of their lives. One Jack Russell living in California is 17 years old, and her owners claim she has as much energy as she had when she was a puppy.

How long do Jack Russells stay puppies?

Some people say that Jack Russells never grow up! They remain active and full of energy long after they reach adulthood, which is two years of age. The primary difference between an adult Jack and a puppy of the breed is that adult Jack Russells have honed their hunting skills and have become more assertive and sometimes even more aggressive.

How active are Jack Russell Terriers?

They are extremely active, possibly more so than any other breed of dog. They never stop moving, are always looking for something to do, and are constantly on the hunt. In fact, Jack Russells are so active and aggressive about finding prey, they often drive their owners crazy and kill or injure other pets. Jacks who don't have an outlet for all their energy often become destructive and will dig up the yard, chew up furniture and bark incessantly.

Jack Russells are the canine equivalent of the Energizer Bunny. They keep going and going and going. A Jack Russell may eventually crash on the couch at the end of the day, but that is only if he has spent that day hunting, running outdoors, chasing balls and generally moving nonstop almost the entire time.

The activity level of the average Jack Russell Terrier is about 10 times that of the average Labrador Retriever, for example. Labs like to run and have fun, but eventually they do sack out on the living room floor. A Jack Russell has to work long and hard before he will have the urge to lie down and sleep for an extended period of time.

Labs also like to take time out to smell the roses. They will kick back and sit at their owner's sides, watching a sunset or gazing at the birds flying overhead. Jack Russells, on the other hand, are hard pressed to sit still for very long. They aren't fans of watching sunsets, and would just as soon catch and eat the birds flying overhead instead of gazing at them.

What are 10 good reasons to want a Jack Russell Terrier?

1. You live on a ranch or a farm and want a dog who will thrive in that kind of environment.

2. You want a dog who will keep rodents, birds and other small animals off your property.

3. You want an intelligent, active dog to compete in dog activities.

4. You want an energetic dog for companionship for outdoor activities.

5. You want an active, entertaining dog with a sense of humor.

6. You have trained dogs in the past, and are looking for a much greater challenge.

7. You want an active dog who will be good around horses.

8. You have a very active outdoor lifestyle and want a dog who can keep up with you.

9. You want an active dog with a cheerful demeanor.

10. You want an affectionate, happy, active dog with plenty of energy and enthusiasm for life.

Why are Jack Russells best suited to life on a ranch or a farm?

There is always something to do on a ranch or farm and plenty of space to run. Jack Russells amuse themselves in such rural environments by hunting for rodents, catching flies, climbing on haystacks, following horses around, tormenting barn cats and stalking cowbirds. They also like to run after other dogs, chase anything that runs past, follow people around and attack moving farm equipment.

This is the kind of constant stimulation the Jack Russell needs to keep him from getting bored.

Why is wanting to get rid of rodents, birds and other small animals a good reason to have a Jack Russell?

Jack Russells live to hunt, and will work tirelessly to capture, kill or chase away any small creature that wanders onto your property. If their prey is underground, they will dig furiously until they unearth the hapless creature. If they can catch a bird, they will, by stalking it like a cat and then running and leaping into the air to catch it. Even when not successful at actually catching birds, Jack Russells do a great job of chasing birds away. Birds quickly learn that any farm or ranch harboring a Jack Russell is not a safe place to be. In fact, just about any animal quickly learns this. Mice and rats will still appear at facilities that have feed and grain stored in sheds and barns, but they will make themselves scarce if there is a Jack Russell Terrier on guard.

Why are Jack Russells good for competing in dog activities?

Speed sports like flyball and agility are perfect for Jack Russells because of the breed's limitless energy and profound drive to perform. Jacks have the nonstop energy and the urge to run and participate in activities that are needed for canine dog sports. It takes a high-energy dog to be successful at these kinds of sports, and Jack Russells are never short on energy or the desire to use it.

Why do Jack Russells make good companions for outdoor activities?

Jack Russells never get tired—*never*. You can hike all day with your Jack Russell and he'll still be up for a game of ball when you get home. You can go camping, and your Jack Russell will try to help you set up your tent. If you go jogging, your Jack will run alongside you tirelessly, and probably pressure you to go even faster. Boating on a lake is another activity enjoyed by Jack Russells, who have no qualms about leaping in to the water to retrieve a tennis ball. Jacks also make great biking companions, and can run alongside a bicycle for miles without getting tired.

Why are Jack Russells so entertaining?

They are natural clowns and are truly fun-loving dogs, up for any kind of activity. They also have funny quirks that can make you laugh. Some of the antics typical of Jack Russells are licking walls, sleeping with all four feet in the air, and tearing around the house, dashing up and over furniture like a maniac, for no apparent reason.

There is something comical about the Jack Russell personality that many people can appreciate. The dog who plays Eddie on *Frasier* is a good example of this. The human actors on the show often play straight man to Eddie's comic antics. One of the reasons Eddie is so funny is because he is a Jack Russell Terrier. His attitude and demeanor lend itself to uproarious laughter.

Why are Jack Russells good dogs for someone who has trained dogs in the past and is looking for a challenge?

Because Jack Russells are difficult to train. They are not like Golden Retrievers, Poodles or Collies, breeds who were bred to pay close attention to their handlers for direction in their work. Instead, Jacks have short attention spans and need a lot of motivation, like a special food or a favorite toy, to stay focused. Even then they can be hard to train because of their very independent nature. They have their own ideas about how things should go, and rarely see the point of listening to what a human has to say, especially if it makes no sense to them.

Why are Jack Russells good around horses?

Jack Russells love horses, especially when those horses are moving. Jacks like to follow horses around the stable and on the trail. They seem to enjoy the company of equines, and horses seem to like them.

Another reason Jack Russells do so well around horses is that stables provide a lot of stimulation for these busy terriers, who always need something to do. Stables have rodents for hunting, and wide open areas to run. People who own horses tend to like Jack Russells because of the breed's toughness and limitless energy. A Jack Russell can follow a horse for miles on a trail ride without getting tired.

The Jack Russell's affinity for horses may also be genetic. Jack Russells were bred in part to run with foxhunters, who hunt on horseback. Being around horses seems to come naturally to their terriers. It could be that a love for horses is in their genes.

Why are Jack Russells good for people with active lifestyles?

People who hike, camp, fish, jog and bike ride on a frequent basis have the kind of lifestyle that best suits the tireless Jack Russell. The breed does best with these kinds of owners because the dog always has something to do and a way to burn energy. Likewise, people with active lifestyles really enjoy being with Jack Russell Terriers. Jacks can always keep up no matter how fast you are going or for how long you've been moving. Active people do not have to baby these dogs, and can be sure that their Jack Russell will be up for just about any outdoor activity they can come up with.

Why do Jack Russells have a cheerful demeanor?

They were simply bred to be that way. Jack Russells are cheerful, happy dogs, always looking for the next bit of fun. In fact, their pursuit of a good time can get them into trouble if they don't have enough to do. They will make their own fun, which might include digging up the backyard or chewing up the coffee table. Or chasing the cat, jumping up on the kitchen table and eating the turkey that is defrosting, tearing a hole through the closed doggy door to get outside and excavating a tunnel under the backyard fence and into the neighbor's yard, and so on.

Do Jack Russell Terriers make good apartment dogs?

Absolutely not. Many people think that because Jack Russells are small, they will do well in an apartment. The truth of the matter is that although they are small, they have too much energy to be confined to a small apartment, especially if there is no yard where they can play and be exercised. A typical Jack Russell Terrier will literally climb the walls of an apartment and go stir crazy. He is likely to start barking incessantly, destroying your furniture, knocking things off shelves and tables (Jack Russells are good jumpers), tearing the curtains off the windows and worse.

Do Jack Russell Terriers make good dogs for a home in the suburbs?

Not usually, unless you have a lot of time to spend exercising the dog. *A lot*. This means a few hours a day of hard exercise, like jogging and ball playing, to tire out a Jack. Don't think leaving the dog out in the backyard alone counts as exercise. You have to actively exercise him to make sure he is exerting himself and that his mind is stimulated. Since most people with jobs don't have that kind of time to devote to exercising a dog, it's not a good idea to have a Jack Russell in the suburbs.

If you try to make this work but don't give the dog enough exercise, he will likely tear up your garden, eat the garden hose, rip potted plants out of their pots, bark all day and worse.

What are 10 bad reasons to want a Jack Russell Terrier?

1. You want a nice, obedient dog like Eddie on *Frasier* or Wishbone on PBS.
2. You want a companion for your pet cat, rabbit or bird.
3. You want a companion for your other small dog.

4. You want a dog to hang out and watch TV with you.

5. You want a small dog who is easy to handle.

6. You have never owned a dog before, and think a Jack Russell would be a good first choice.

7. You are not an experienced dog trainer, but want a dog you can teach to do all kinds of tricks.

8. You want a dog for your young children.

9. You work all day, but think a small dog like a Jack Russell Terrier will do fine being at home alone all day while you are gone.

10. You don't know much about the breed but are sure you want one because they are so cute.

But Eddie on *Frasier* and Wishbone on PBS are obedient. Why wouldn't my Jack Russell be?

Because you most likely don't have several hours a day to spend training and exercising your Jack Russell, nor do you have the expertise of a professional trainer. Also, these dogs might be well behaved while they are on TV, but their time in front of the camera is limited. The rest of the day, they are running around and being typical Jack Russell Terriers.

Why can't my Jack Russell be a companion for my pet cat, rabbit or bird?

Your Jack Russell doesn't see himself as a companion to small animals. He sees himself as hunter who was put on this earth to kill such creatures. Jacks are relentless when it comes to hunting, and view small animals as something to hunt, not play with. Your terrier will take one look at your rabbit or bird and begin trying to figure out how he can get to the animal to kill it. He may not attack your cat right away, but in time he will likely decide that kitty is prey too. At the very least, your Jack Russell will harass your small pets. At the worst, he will kill them. This is especially true of small rodents like hamsters, mice, rats, gerbils and guinea pigs. Never, ever expose a Jack Russell to these kinds of pets. Tragedy is sure to result.

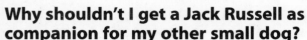
Why shouldn't I get a Jack Russell as companion for my other small dog?

Generally speaking, Jack Russells don't really like other dogs. They view them as competition for food and attention. In the worst case scenario, the Jack Russell will decide to act on the notion that he'd prefer to be an only dog and will start fighting with your other dog to get him or her to submit. The fighting will escalate to the point of sure disaster, especially if the other dog is likely to fight back rather than be submissive and kowtow to the Jack Russell's every whim.

Most terriers don't get along with other dogs, but Jack Russells are particularly disagreeable in this regard. It doesn't matter how big the other dog is, either. Even though Jack Russells are small, they see themselves as large and often bully other dogs, both large and small.

In situations where a small dog does not back down quickly enough from a Jack Russell, that dog's life is in danger. Jack Russells have been known to kill small dogs, even dogs they have lived with for years.

Why aren't Jack Russells a good dog to hang out and watch TV with you?

Jack Russells have way too much energy to be couch potatoes. The only way a Jack Russell might be content to sit and watch TV with you is if it's nighttime and you spent the entire day making him run by throwing a ball to him for hours on end, or taking him along on a very long bike ride. Or if you live on a farm and your terrier has been outside hunting, climbing and digging all day, he might be willing to crash out on the couch in the evening. But these are the only scenarios where you'll have a Jack Russell behave in couch potato mode. More likely, you can expect your Jack Russell to be running around the house getting into trouble while you are trying to relax in front of the television.

The Jack Russell is a small dog, so wouldn't it be an easy dog to handle?

No. The Jack Russell's small size is deceptive. The Jack Russell is a big dog in a small body and has more energy and tenacity than most large breeds. Think of the Jack Russell as the Tasmanian Devil in the Bugs Bunny cartoons. Taz is small, but he's like a tornado. That is the Jack Russell Terrier.

Some people think that they can bully a small dog into behaving simply because that dog is smaller than they are. Jack Russells are surprisingly strong for their size, and can get nasty if they are treated roughly. Jack Russells won't hesitate to bite to defend themselves if someone is trying to push them around.

Why isn't the Jack Russell a good choice for a first dog?

Because Jack Russells are aggressive in nature, extremely active and hard to train. Most people who have never had a dog before are completely overwhelmed by a Jack Russell Terrier. If you are looking for a first-time dog, you are better off with a breed like the Labrador Retriever or the Golden Retriever. If you want a small dog who is easy to handle, try a Toy Poodle or Pomeranian. Trying to tackle a Jack Russell Terrier as your first dog is likely to make you give up dogs forever.

Why can't I teach my Jack Russell all kinds of tricks even though I'm not an experienced dog trainer?

Jack Russells are difficult to train. They don't listen well, and have their own ideas about what they should be doing with their time. In order to overcome this, you need experience and knowledge as a dog trainer. It takes plenty of creativity as a trainer to get a Jack's attention and keep it, and to convince a Jack Russell that he should listen to anything you say at all. (For more information, see Chapter 7, What's Involved in Training a Jack Russell Terrier?)

Why isn't the Jack Russell Terrier a good dog for young children?

Jack Russells don't put up with the kind of treatment young kids typically dish out. Small children often pull tails, tug on ears and step on paws, without realizing they are hurting the dog. Many dogs, like Labrador Retrievers and Golden Retrievers, will tolerate this kind of behavior because they sense that the small humans who are tormenting them are simply younger versions of adult humans and don't really know what they are doing. Jack Russells don't see it that way, however. Jacks don't care how old the small human is and don't seem to recognize the innocence of a child. They simply will not put up with tail pulling and ear pinching and all the other things that small children do to dogs. They have no qualms about biting a small child to get the point of "leave me alone" across.

Can I leave a Jack Russell Terrier alone at all?

Only if you have him confined to a secure crate, and then not for more than a few hours a day. Plus, you can only do this if you have given the Jack Russell several hours of hard, interactive exercise before you leave. You will have to exercise the heck out of him when you come back, too, since he'll be raring to go once you let him out of that crate. (For more information about using a crate, see Chapter 7, What's Involved in Training a Jack Russell Terrier?)

Can't I just leave the Jack Russell outside while I'm not home?

Not unless you want your garden destroyed, your lawn furniture eaten, holes dug under your fence and angry neighbors who have been listening to loud barking for hours on end. Also, if you don't have a secure fence, your Jack Russell will quickly find a way to escape, whether that is over it, under it or around it.

Why shouldn't I get a Jack Russell because they are cute? Isn't that a good reason to get a breed?

It's tempting to get a dog because it's cute, but that's never a good reason alone to pick a breed. The way a dog looks is only a small part of who that dog is. Personality of the breed should be your uppermost concern if you want to live a happy life with your dog.

Jack Russells may look cute, but they are high-maintenance dogs who are difficult to train and manage. They might look like stuffed toys, but their appearance truly belies their personalities. They are tough, tenacious little dogs who are very difficult to handle.

What are the top 10 reasons people give up their Jack Russell Terriers?

1. "The dog destroys things in the house."
2. "The dog digs up the yard."
3. "The dog barks all the time when we're not home."
4. "The dog demands too much of our time and attention."
5. "The dog is not good with our children and other pets."
6. "The dog is disobedient and won't listen to us."
7. "We are moving, and can't take the dog."
8. "We thought we were getting a small dog who would sit on our laps, but this dog won't sit still."
9. "The dog goes to the bathroom in the house."
10. "The dog keeps running away."

Why do people have all these problems with Jack Russells?

Because they didn't really know what kind of dog the Jack Russell was before they got one. Jacks are high-energy dogs who need a vast amount of exercise, stimulation and training. Most of the problems people have with Jack Russell Terriers are the result of poor planning on the part of the owners and a lack of training of the dogs. People just don't realize Jack Russells really are so active and hard to train. This breed is not for everyone. In fact, they aren't for most people. Most Jack Russell Terriers who are abandoned or surrendered to animal shelters were given up because the owners underestimated or simply didn't know how difficult life would be with one of these tenacious terriers.

Do Jack Russell Terriers bark very much?

Jack Russells bark when they are excited, when they are bored and when they are hunting. Seeing the mail carrier or even a kid riding a bike down the street is usually enough to set off a lot of barking in a Jack Russell. Jack Russells left alone in the house or yard with nothing to do will bark out of sheer boredom and will do it loudly and obsessively. If a Jack Russell has cornered an animal when hunting, the dog will bark at that creature out of sheer excitement.

Why do Jack Russells bark so often?

They were bred to bark whenever they cornered their prey underground to let the hunter know their location. Jack Russells still retain that strong tendency to bark, and apply this tendency to many different situations.

Are Jack Russells hard to house-train?

Yes, they are often very difficult to house-train. They require a lot of patience as well as positive reinforcement like food or play to convince them they should go to the bathroom outside the house and not in it. The reason for this is that they simply march to their own drummer. A Jack Russell sees no reason to hold his urine or feces for when he's outdoors. Why not go in the house where it's most convenient? The fact that his owner doesn't appreciate soiled carpeting or a pile of poop in the living room doesn't really matter much to the typical Jack Russell Terrier.

In order to get a Jack Russell to see the wisdom of pottying outside, owners have to use a lot of rewards. Eventually, the Jack Russell will decide that going to the bathroom outdoors is more beneficial than doing it inside, because treats and/or play results when he does his business in the yard instead of in the house. In time, going potty outdoors will simply become a habit.

How big do Jack Russells get?

Jack Russells vary a lot in size, depending on the type of Jack Russell. The smallest members of the breed stand only about 10 inches at the shoulder.

The largest Jack Russells measure around 15 inches high. Small Jack Russells can weigh as little as 10 pounds, while larger individuals reach 15 pounds.

Do Jack Russells shed?

Yes, they shed a lot. The broken-coated type of Jack Russell also requires professional grooming in order to keep his coat looking tidy.

What kind of coats do Jack Russells have?

This depends on the breed standard of each of the two Jack Russell Terrier clubs. The Parson Russell Terrier Association of America (PRTAA) recognizes a smooth-coated and a broken-coated Jack Russell. The PRTAA describes the smooth coat as coarse and waterproof, and flat but hard while being dense and abundant. The club describes the broken coat as a double coat that is coarse and waterproof, with a short, dense undercoat covered with a harsh, straight, tight "jacket" (the area covering the upper back and rib cage) that lies flat and close to the body and legs of the dog.

The Jack Russell Terrier Club of America (JRTCA) also recognizes a smooth coat, and describes it as smooth without being so sparse as not to provide a certain amount of protection from the elements and undergrowth (brush). They also recognize a rough or broken coat, and describe it as rough without being wooly.

What is a breed standard?

Each Jack Russell club has a blueprint of what a perfect Jack Russell Terrier should look like. Of course there is no such thing as a perfect Jack Russell or a perfect anything, but the standard provides something for breeders to shoot for.

The breed standard is used in dog shows to help the judge determine if the dog he or she is judging is a good example of the breed. A judge will look at the part of the breed standard that describes coat, for example, and then decide if the dog in the show ring adequately fits the description in the standard for coat.

Are Jack Russells friendly with strangers?

Not usually. In fact, they can be possessive of "their" people and property and can be aggressive toward strangers. This is not true of all Jack Russells, however. Some are happy to receive visitors, while others would just as soon chew up anyone who sets foot on their property.

Isn't being unfriendly toward strangers a good thing? I don't want someone to break into my house.

Jack Russells make good watchdogs, meaning they will bark long and loud if someone is approaching your house. That's good because they can alert you to an approaching stranger long before you would hear or see that person yourself. But Jacks don't always distinguish between someone you want in your house and someone you don't. Your Jack Russell is just as likely to bark like a maniac at your Uncle Fred from Iowa who is coming up the driveway to ring your doorbell as he would be at a criminal who is scoping out your house for a robbery. Know that this protective attitude about Uncle Fred may continue even after your uncle has come into your home with your permission. If your Jack Russell bites Uncle Fred or anyone else who comes to your home with your permission, you will be both embarrassed and legally liable.

2

How Does a Jack Russell Terrier Behave?

How do Jack Russell Terriers behave as pets? • What is *temperament* and why is it important? • What if my Jack Russell doesn't see me as the leader? • What is the general temperament of Jack Russell Terriers? • How can I determine a particular Jack Russell puppy's temperament before I buy him or her? • How are Jack Russells with children? • How are Jack Russell Terriers with the elderly? • Are Jack Russells good watchdogs? • What kinds of people will best be able to develop a Jack Russell into a good pet? • What's the best way to try to interpret what my Jack Russell is conveying? • What are some physical cues that will help me understand my Jack Russell's behavior? • What can I do in and around my home to make my dog's behavior more acceptable? • What causes a dog to become aggressive? • What causes a Jack Russell to be destructive? • What causes nuisance barking? • What causes Jack Russells to dig obsessively? • I have a friend whose Jack Russell is nothing like the dogs described here. Why is that?

How do Jack Russell Terriers behave as pets?

Often badly, if they are not trained and exercised a lot, or if mismatched with their owners. Jack Russell Terriers represent a combination of high energy, curiosity and tenacity. They are always on the go, and always in search of something to do. Sometimes, in their quest, they can get into trouble.

Why are Jack Russells so tenacious?

When a Jack Russell sees something he wants, he goes for it and not much can stop him. Whether it's a toy, the neighbor's cat, a sock you dropped on the floor or your pet canary, if your Jack Russell wants it, he is going to find a way to get it.

They were bred to be this way! Only a tenacious dog makes a good hunter of small game. Animals such as foxes, mice, rats and gophers will do whatever they have to do in order to escape a chasing, digging terrier. If the dog is going to be successful as a hunter, he has to be the kind of dog who doesn't give up easily.

Why is exercise so important for a well-behaved Jack Russell Terrier?

Because Jack Russells were bred to hunt all day, every day, they have incredible energy and need an outlet for it. If you don't give them one, they will find another way to expend that energy. Chances are, it won't be something you appreciate.

Your Jack Russell needs rigorous exercise for several hours a day. This means jogging, playing ball and hiking. Participating in sports like agility, flyball and earthdog trials are also great ways not only to exercise your Jack Russell, but also to provide mental stimulation. The combination will result in a more well-behaved Jack Russell Terrier.

What is *temperament* and why is it important?

Temperament is the dog's nature and personality, and is often inherited. Dogs can have dominant temperaments, medium temperaments or submissive temperaments. Dogs with dominant temperaments are harder to train and sometimes have problems with aggression, especially toward other dogs. Medium temperaments are the easiest to train and live with, while submissive temperaments can be very sensitive and sometimes fearful.

Temperament can also be affected by early experiences. A puppy who is handled often and is well socialized will have a more stable temperament than one who grows up in isolation.

Why do dogs have different temperaments?

The domesticated dog is a descendent of the wolf. Dogs inherited temperament traits from these ancestors. Wolf packs need leaders in order to function efficiently in the wild. The top wolf makes decisions for the group. In wolf packs, leaders and followers are determined by the individual wolf's temperament. Domestic dogs like your Jack Russell Terrier see their human families as packs. The goal is for your dog to view you as the leader, not himself. Otherwise, behavior problems can surface.

What if my Jack Russell doesn't see me as the leader?

Then he will make himself the leader. Every pack needs someone to be in charge, and if it's not you or someone else in your family, then your Jack Russell will put himself at the top. It is his instinctive nature to see to it that there is a definite pecking order within his "pack"— namely, your household. If your dog sees himself as the leader, he will start bossing you around and trying to run the household. He will growl at you, snap at you and possibly even bite if you don't do what he wants. In his eyes, you are his follower and should heed his commands.

He will assert himself in all types of social interactions and activities. He won't let you move around when he is sleeping in the bed with you. He won't let you displace him from the sofa or from his bed. He won't let you near his food bowl. He won't allow people to stand up after they have been sitting in a chair. And the list goes on.

What is the general temperament of Jack Russell Terriers?

Most Jack Russell Terriers possess dominant temperaments, although this varies from individual to individual. Terrier breeds are typically more on the dominant side, particularly Jack Russell Terriers.

Why are Jack Russell Terriers usually dominant?

They need this kind of temperament to hunt small game. Certain animals like foxes and badgers will fight back when cornered. A successful hunting dog will be dominant enough to fight back and to stay with the hunt and not run away in the face of danger.

How does a dominant dog act?

Dominant dogs tend to be independent, willful and often aggressive with other dogs and sometimes with people. The classic signs of a dominant Jack Russell include ears forward, tail up and stiff and barely wagging, body tense and leaning forward, hair up on shoulders and spine, prolonged staring and teeth bared in the front of the mouth. They can also be harder to train, and will often "test" you to see who is the boss.

How will my Jack Russell test me?

Your Jack Russell may test you in various ways. He may growl at you when you try to move him off the bed or ignore you when you call him.

What do I do if my Jack Russell behaves this way?

If you have established yourself as the leader, a strong, firm word should be enough to remind your Jack Russell who is in charge. If this doesn't work, seek the advice of a professional trainer who is experienced with terriers and can help you change the pecking order in your household. You need to take immediate action to prevent this behavior from continuing.

How can I determine a particular Jack Russell puppy's temperament before I buy him or her?

Talk to the breeder first and ask him or her to help you evaluate the temperament of the puppies in the litter. No one knows the puppies better than the breeder. If you want a dog who is less dominant and more medium in temperament (many people believe medium temperament is ideal for pets), ask the breeder to select a puppy of this description from the litter. Be aware that it may be difficult to find a Jack Russell with a medium temperament.

How does the breeder evaluate the puppy's temperament?

By observing the puppy with his littermates, and by performing a puppy temperament test that enables the breeder to assess the degree of dominance in the litter of puppies.

What is a puppy temperament test?

A puppy temperament test is a series of steps that help determine a pup's personality at a young age. The test should be performed at seven weeks of age, and with the breeder's permission and assistance.

Most experienced breeders know how to administer a puppy temperament test. If they do not, look for another, better-qualified breeder to obtain your puppy.

How much exercise does my Jack Russell need?

More than the average dog. You should spend at least two hours a day giving your dog hard exercise that requires him to run at full speed. That means making him run and run and run, for as long as you can.

How will my active Jack Russell feel about being confined while boarded?

He won't be happy about it, which is why you should make provisions to have your dog taken out of his cage and played with as many times as possible during the day. This may cost extra, but your dog needs it.

How are Jack Russells with children?

Jack Russells are usually okay with older kids as long as the dog has been exposed to children from puppyhood and the children treat the dog with respect. This breed doesn't do as well with children under the age of six because Jacks are generally not tolerant of small children and won't forgive the kinds of transgressions that young kids are often guilty of committing toward dogs, such as ear pulling or stepping on paws. Regardless of the child's age, supervision is mandatory when kids are handling Jack Russell Terriers.

What do I need to do to make sure my Jack Russell Terrier and my children get along well, and that there is no danger to the child or the dog when they are together?

Never leave them alone together. Also, make sure your kids are old enough (six and up) and that they interact with your Jack Russell while he is still a young puppy. Be careful to make sure that all of your dog's experiences with children are positive. Teach your children to have respect for your dog, and not to pick him up and carry him around or bother him when he's sleeping. In turn, do not let your Jack Russell engage in aggressive games like tug-of-war or play biting with your kids. Also, don't allow your Jack Russell to snatch food away from your children. If your children are old enough (six or older), have them attend obedience classes with you and your dog so they can learn how to interact properly with the dog. If your kids participate in your Jack Russell's obedience training, this will help your dog see your children as authority figures in the household.

Why is it important that my Jack Russell see my kids as authority figures?

So he will respect them. Otherwise, he'll start trying to push them around by growling and possibly even snapping at them, just as he would a dog whom he views as a subordinate.

How are Jack Russell Terriers with the elderly?

Jack Russells are often too boisterous and energetic for most elderly people to deal with. An untrained Jack Russell can be particularly bothersome, since behaviors like jumping up and play biting can be particularly unacceptable to seniors.

How are Jack Russells with people who are not part of the family?

Sometimes okay, sometimes not. Properly trained Jack Russells learn that nonfamily members who are welcomed by you should be accepted into the household without a fuss. Your Jack Russell will bark when a friend comes to the front door, but he should greet that person happily once it's obvious that you have invited the person into your house. It's important to note that some Jacks are very protective of one or more family members, and can behave aggressively toward people they don't know, even if you have welcomed that person into your home.

Are Jack Russells good watchdogs?

Yes! Jack Russells make great watchdogs, and will bark loudly when someone is approaching or has entered your property. However, they cannot be relied upon as effective guard dogs because of their small size, although they will certainly try to attack an intruder.

What kinds of people will best be able to develop a Jack Russell into a good pet?

Only energetic, patient people with an active lifestyle, a sense of humor, experience with dogs and the willingness to train a challenging breed. The Jack Russell's intense energy and independence require substantial energy and dedication in return on the part of an owner. No Jack Russell can be completely controlled, and successful Jack Russell owners are the type of people who can live with this reality. In fact, many Jack Russell people actually like this aspect of the Jack Russell's personality and appreciate the breed's independence and energy.

What kinds of people will probably have difficulty managing a Jack Russell Terrier as a pet?

People who have not researched the breed and don't realize the high activity level of the Jack Russell Terrier will have difficulty managing this dog. People who lead busy lives with little time to exercise a very active dog will have problems. So will sedentary people who are looking for a canine couch potato to keep them company. Jack Russells are anything but couch potatoes. Also, anyone who lives in an apartment will have trouble with a Jack Russell Terrier. People who are not willing to attend obedience classes and put substantial energy into training a dog will not be happy with a Jack Russell Terrier as a pet. First-time dog owners also have trouble handling this active terrier.

What's the best way to try to interpret what my Jack Russell is conveying?

Learn not to focus on just one part of your dog's body. You've got to look at the whole package and size up the situation to accurately interpret what your dog is telling you.

The first step is to step back and study how your Jack Russell communicates with other dogs. Dog-to-dog "chat" is often silent. When dogs first meet, they can quickly size up each other without a single bark. They sniff each other, eye each other, and within seconds know each other's sex, age, health condition and where they stand on the canine hierarchy. Each canine "reads" the total head-to-tail messages being delivered.

What are some physical cues that will help me understand my Jack Russell's behavior?

Remember not to rely on just one body language cue when "reading" your dog, and that some of these signs may not be so easily noticed among some breeds:

- **Ears:** Be aware of ears that are erect, tense and leaning forward. This usually indicates a challenging or assertive dog. Calm, contented dogs tend to relax the muscle tension around their ears. Fearful or worried dogs often pull their ears back against their heads.

- **Eyes:** Direct staring, by you or a dog, means confidence and possibly dominance. Dogs who look at you and then look away are indicating that they are yielding power to you. Dogs who greet you with "soft eyes" are contented. Dogs with dilated large pupils when the light of the day should make them smaller are either fearful or aggressive.

- **Mouth:** Lip curling and exposing teeth may be a sign of aggression in a dominant breed like a Jack Russell but a sign of pure happiness in other breeds like Chesapeake Bay Retrievers. Tongue flicking often means a feelings of uncertainty and uneasiness. Yawning usually symbolizes stress, not fatigue. Yawning helps lower a dog's blood pressure to help him stay calm. Dogs who mouth your hand without using their teeth are delivering a friendly greeting, but dogs who use their teeth are challenging your authority. Even friendly mouthing should be discouraged as it can lead to aggressive biting in dominant dogs.

- **Torso tension:** Muscle tension is your barometer to the emotions being conveyed by a dog. Tightened muscles, especially around the head and shoulders, often indicate a dog who is scared or aggressive.

- **Gestures:** Play bowing (front torso down, front legs extended, back torso up and tail wagging) is the universal canine sign for happiness and an invitation to play. Nose nudging is a plea for affection or a cue that you're in his chair and please move. Paw lifting often means "let's play" or "pay attention to me."

- **Fur:** A calm dog displays a smooth coat from his shoulders to his hips. A scared or challenged dog will elevate the hairs (called hackles) along his spine to appear larger in size.

- **Tail:** An alert dog keeps his tail tall and erect. A fearful dog will tuck his tail between his legs. An excited dog will hoist his tail up and wag it quickly from side to side. A cautious dog will hold his tail straight out and wag it slowly and steadily. A contented dog will keep his tail relaxed and at ease.

What are some signs to look for to see if my Jack Russell is submissive?

- The ears are back or flattened against the head.
- The tail is down or tucked between the legs.
- The weight is shifted to the back legs.
- The head is lowered.
- He makes indirect eye contact and quick glances are evident.
- The lips are pulled back in a submissive grin.
- He may roll over and expose his belly.
- He may crouch down and urinate.

What are some signs to look for to see if my Jack Russell is happy and relaxed?

- All four feet are placed evenly on the ground, or the dog is sitting.
- The posture is free of muscle tension.
- The forehead is smooth.

- The eyes are narrowed or half closed in a relaxed manner.
- The mouth is relaxed at the corners or partly open as if smiling.
- Floppy-eared breeds will let ears hang loosely, while breeds with pricked ears will let them fall slightly outward.

What are som\e signs to look for to see if my Jack Russell is worried or anxious?

- The pupils are dilated.
- The mouth is open.
- The lips are pulled back and creased at the corners.
- The dog may be panting, a sure sign of stress.
- The forehead muscle is tight, with ears pulled back against the head.
- The dog may yawn repeatedly.

My Jack Russell Terrier is quite vocal but he seems to make different sounds at different times. What's he saying?

A dog's vocabulary is limited, but the sounds are consistent in their meaning, according to animal behavior experts. Here is a rundown of the most common canine vocalizations:

- **High-pitched bark.** A dog is lonely or worried.
- **Quick, high-pitched repetitive barks.** A dog wants to play or give chase.
- **Low, repetitive barks.** A dog feels protective or defensive toward the approach of a stranger.
- **A single bark or two.** A dog is saying, "Hey! I'm here and interested in what you're doing."
- **Growling with teeth exposed and tense body leaning forward.** This is a verbal warning to back off.
- **Growling with body crouched low.** A dog is telling you he is feeling defensive or afraid.

- **Sing-song howling.** This is a dog's version of the telephone. Howling is used to contact other dogs.
- **Squeaky, repetitive yaps or whines.** A dog speaks this way when he feels worried, scared or stressed.

What can I do in and around my home to make my dog's behavior more acceptable?

The first important step is to Jack Russell Terrier–proof your home. Reduce the number of "opportunities" your Jack Russell can discover that will get him into trouble and cause havoc in your home. Think of your dog as a curious two-year-old. Go through your home room by room and look for any items that may harm your dog. Prevent accidental poisoning by installing childproof plastic latches on kitchen and bathroom cabinet doors, keeping plants out of reach, and not allowing your dog access to the garage, where he can lick spilled antifreeze or other dangerous chemicals. Keep the lid down on toilets and keep candy jars, loose coins and jewelry out of paw's reach.

Okay, my house is doggy-proofed. What's next?

Tap into your Jack Russell's inquisitive nature and drive to stay busy. When you're home and can't keep a constant eye on your dog, keep him occupied in a healthy way by offering him a hollow, hard rubber, chewable toy stuffed with his favorite treat: peanut butter, cream cheese, mashed bananas, pieces of rice cake or pieces of kibble. Your dog will be happily working at getting every little morsel. This tactic helps curb destructiveness, overeager greeting and separation anxiety tendencies.

Provide your Jack Russell with plenty of mental and physical exercise outlets. Schedule at least 20 minutes before you go to work and add some spice to walking your dog. A lot of destructive behavior is due to a dog who is bored or one who receives inadequate amounts of exercise. When you take your dog out on a walk, don't bring him back in once he goes to the bathroom. Spend time and practice such commands as "heel," "sit" and "roll over." You are reinforcing your dog's mental focus and giving him a good workout so that when he comes inside, your Jack Russell is ready to relax or take a nap.

What causes a dog to become aggressive?

Jack Russells tend to be naturally dominant dogs because they were bred to be spunky and tenacious. If you put a dog with a personality like this together with an owner who does not take control of the dog's behavior with training and constant reinforcement of who is the leader, the dog may become aggressive. Dogs can be aggressive when they see themselves as the leader of the pack. They use aggressive behavior to keep everyone else "in line."

Some dogs also develop aggressiveness as a reaction to fear. Known as fear biters, these dogs will attack when they feel threatened. Such dogs do not feel secure in their home, in part because they do not feel that there is a leader taking care of them.

What do I do if my Jack Russell becomes aggressive?

Aggression is a serious problem in dogs, even in a small breed like the Jack Russell. A growl eventually leads to a bite, so it's a good idea to get help the minute you see any kind of aggressive behavior from your dog. Call a professional trainer or an animal behaviorist, and work with this professional to solve your dog's aggression problem before it's too late and he bites someone.

How do I keep my Jack Russell from becoming aggressive?

Buy your dog from a reputable breeder who has evaluated the puppy's temperament and has determined that the pup does not have a tendency toward aggression. Then do your part by taking your Jack Russell to obedience classes and working hard to establish your leadership with your dog. Reinforce your dog's training throughout his life to reduce the dog's inclination to "test" you to see if you are still the leader.

What causes a Jack Russell to be destructive?

Usually boredom and lack of something productive to do are generally the situations that lead to destructiveness. This behavior can also be a symptom of separation anxiety.

What is separation anxiety?

Some dogs become anxious when separated from their owners while left alone. Dogs who are anxious don't know what to do with themselves, so they start chewing and tearing at things in their environment. When dogs are indoors, the furniture and carpeting often get the most heat. Dogs kept outdoors will bark incessantly and dig up the yard. They may even try to escape.

What should I do if my dog is suffering from separation anxiety?

You can do a few things to help remedy his anxiety. First, confine him while you are gone. Dogs feel more secure when they are in a crate or small space than they do with the run of the house or backyard. Give him a favorite toy that is only given to him when he's crated. Put a television or radio on while you are gone so your dog hears human voices. This may calm him. You can also ask a friend, neighbor or professional pet sitter to come to your house in your absence to take your dog for a walk or a game of ball outside.

If all this fails, talk to a professional trainer, animal behaviorist or your veterinarian. In extreme cases, dogs can take anti-depressant medications to help with their anxiety.

How can I prevent my dog from developing separation anxiety?

Teach him to be alone when he is a puppy by leaving him in his crate for short amounts of time with a chew toy or a dog biscuit. Help him learn to feel okay when he's alone. If you have an adult dog, leave him alone for short periods of time after giving him something he can eat or chew on while you are gone. You want him to associate your absence with something soothing, like food.

What causes nuisance barking?

Jack Russells were bred to bark when their prey was cornered to let the hunter know where they were. Consequently, this breed likes to bark. When Jack Russells get bored, one of the first things they do is start barking continually. Barking gives them an outlet for their pent-up energy and helps to relieve boredom. Unfortunately, your neighbors won't appreciate your Jack Russell's methods of amusing himself.

Dogs who suffer from separation anxiety can also develop nuisance barking as a way to help relieve stress.

What do I do if my Jack Russell is nuisance barking?

Most Jack Russells do this when they are bored, so figure out why your dog is going so stir crazy that he is giving voice on a constant basis. If you have him out in the backyard alone all day, he is probably lonely and miserable and is barking to relieve some of his anxiety. Instead, crate him in the house while you're not home, or get someone to come in and play with him during the day. Also, count your blessings that all your Jack Russell is doing is barking all day. He could also take to destroying your yard, since bored dogs often do things like this when they are unhappy.

How do I prevent my Jack Russell from developing the problem of nuisance barking?

By always giving him something to do, and confining him to a crate when you aren't home. Remember not to keep him in his crate for more than a few hours at a time, and give him plenty of hard exercise before confining him.

What causes Jack Russells to dig obsessively?

Jack Russell Terriers were bred to hunt underground, and some of them can be pernicious diggers because their instinct to dig is so strong. A dog like this can make short work of your backyard in no time.

Other reasons Jacks will dig are out of boredom or to get at a rodent that has gone into an underground burrow.

What do I do if my Jack Russell is an obsessive digger?

If he's digging out of boredom, give him more exercise and something to do instead of excavating your yard. If he does it when you're not home, keep him confined to a crate where he can't get into trouble.

You can also teach your Jack Russell to dig on command. Create an area where he can dig to his heart's content. Some trainers believe that teaching a dog to do an existing behavior when you tell him to will decrease the likelihood that he will do it at random on his own.

I have a friend whose Jack Russell is nothing like the dogs described here. Why is that?

Dogs are individuals, just like people, and Jack Russells are no exception. While the personality traits described in this book are typical of the Jack Russell Terrier breed, there can be exceptions. Stories are told about quiet, mellow Jack Russells who would never harm a fly and prefer to lie around the house and do nothing. Keep in mind that these dogs are the exception to the rule. When you get a Jack Russell Terrier, you are more likely find yourself with a busy, feisty little dog with a big-dog attitude.

3

How Will My Jack Russell Terrier Grow and Develop?

 How can I expect my Jack Russell to develop during his first year? • What is my Jack Russell capable of learning as a young puppy? • When is the best age to remove a Jack Russell puppy from his mother and littermates and bring him home? • What can I expect from my Jack Russell puppy between three and six months of age? • Why is socialization with other dogs and with people so important at this age for Jack Russell Terrier puppies? • Why is this age often called the "juvenile period" and what can I expect? • How do Jack Russells develop physically between six and nine months of age? • How do Jack Russells develop physically and mentally between 9 and 12 months of age? • What can I expect from an adult Jack Russell Terrier? • At what age is a Jack Russell considered a senior? • What should I do to help my senior Jack Russell live a comfortable life?

How can I expect my Jack Russell to develop during his first year?

By your Jack Russell's first birthday, he should be 95 percent adult-like in physique, intelligence and attitude. For dogs, complete social maturity, depending on the breed, usually occurs within 18 to 24 months. Jack Russells, like other small breeds, develop physically more quickly than larger breeds. For example, a Jack Russell should reach its adult weight of 10 to 15 pounds by nine to 10 months. In contrast, a German Shepherd often requires 18 months to reach an expected adult weight of 75 pounds. Proper socialization, a nutritionally balanced diet and regular medical exams combine to improve a puppy's chance of growing into a healthy, happy and well-socialized adult.

Why is it so important to spend quality time with him, especially during his first year?

Time spent together helps him bond with you, and helps teach him how to be a well-behaved dog. A common reason so many young Jack Russell Terriers and other highly active breeds are relinquished to animal shelters is because some people don't realize their roles in properly socializing and training their puppies. You need to understand what your puppy's needs are and what is considered normal puppy behavior during the first year. The sooner you can introduce fun and positive learning to your puppy, the less likely you'll have to deal with serious behavior problems when he becomes an adult.

What is typical Jack Russell puppy behavior?

Lots of running, jumping, barking, biting, chewing and playing. Jack Russell Terriers are little balls of energy who literally bounce off the walls. Your puppy will run around during his waking moments, looking for things to play with, like toys, people and other animals. He will chew on things, dig in the dirt and jump up on furniture. Then he will suddenly fall asleep. He will nap sporadically during the day. He should sleep through the night and wake with as much energy as he had the day before—maybe even more.

How should I handle this behavior?

Give him plenty of chew toys, balls and interaction. This is a good time to start teaching him how he should behave in the house and in your yard. Remember, whatever you let him do as a puppy he will continue to do as an adult. Teach him not to bite people's hands or clothing, or the furniture or plants, by stating a firm "no" and ignoring him for a few minutes right after he commits the offense. When he finally crashes and falls asleep, leave him alone and let him get his rest. Use that time to get stuff done around the house, because when he wakes up, you'll have your hands full once again.

What is my Jack Russell capable of learning as a young puppy?

Puppies are eager and willing to learn all kinds of things at a young age. They can learn basic obedience commands and household rules like potty training and no biting. You can start teaching your puppy fun tricks at the age of six months.

What kind of exercise and how much will my Jack Russell puppy need?

As much as you can give him, for as long as he wants it. This will add up to at least three hours a day or more, depending on your particular Jack Russell. Each dog is an individual, and some puppies have more energy than others. Play games with him of "fetch the ball" and "chase the toy" (tie twine to a stuffed dog toy and drag it around). Teach him to sit and come using treats for mental stimulation. If your Jack Russell is over the age of 18 weeks, you can take him on walks or to a dog park for exercise if your vet says it's okay. Or, if you have a friend with a puppy who is healthy and has gotten his shots, you can ask the friend to come over so the puppies can play. This is a great way to socialize your Jack Russell with other dogs.

What kind of training will my puppy need? How much is he ready for, and when?

He needs basic obedience training where he will learn how to come when called, sit, lie down and do other behaviors on command. He also needs to learn the rules of the house, including potty training. All this can start from the first day you get him home. Teach him to sit and to come when you call him. When you start obedience classes, you will learn how to teach him to lie down and perform other actions when you ask him to. (For more information on obedience training, see Chapter 7, What's Involved in Training a Jack Russell Terrier?)

When is the best age to remove a Jack Russell puppy from his mother and littermates and bring him home?

Your breeder should not separate the puppy from his mother or littermates until after eight weeks when he is fully weaned. Puppies are much more balanced temperament-wise when they remain with their mothers and/or siblings until at least eight weeks of age. Puppies taken away sooner are more likely to be fearful, hyperactive or even fear aggressive, but veterinary researchers still can't scientifically explain why. It is also important to be ready to bring home a young puppy. Learn about how to handle the youngster's upbringing before you bring him into your home.

How hard could it be to take care of a young Jack Russell Terrier puppy?

Puppies take a lot of work to raise correctly. In many ways, they are just like babies. The more attention that you pay them as puppies and arrange for them to experience pleasant and happy circumstances, the more they will develop into happy, well-adjusted adults. Get your puppy used to having his belly rubbed, his ears and paws touched and his mouth examined. These steps will make the trip to the veterinarian's office far less traumatic and will make him more able to cope with the kinds of situations that everyday life poses for a dog.

Expose your puppy to lots of different people and different settings (car rides, a friend's home, a park) once he is old enough to have had his third set of shots, and to different stimuli (vacuum cleaner noise, kitchen cooking smells and friendly older dogs). By age 10 to 12 weeks, if your vet gives permission, enroll your puppy in an organized obedience class with other puppies to further hone his social development and learning.

What are some physical developments to expect by the time a Jack Russell Terrier is eight weeks old?

A puppy's vision should be completely developed by eight weeks. With a mouthful of baby teeth, a puppy is able to eat commercial puppy food. A puppy is also able to identify his mother, littermates and members of the household by sight, smell and sound. This is a time of rapid physical growth as a puppy progresses from walking to full-stride running, rolling and playful wrestling. By this time, most puppies have the neuromuscular development to be able to control their bladders long enough to urinate outside the sleeping area in more appropriate places, like outside.

What can I expect from my Jack Russell puppy between three and six months of age?

Your puppy will be full of energy and will never stop moving during the period of his development. He'll be teething much of that time, and will try to chew on everything he can get his mouth on. He will also be developing a strong bond with you and members of your family.

What will be happening to my puppy physically during these three months?

Your Jack Russell puppy's body is getting more adult-like, and he should be able to sleep through the night without having a potty accident. His permanent teeth will begin coming in between 5 and 6 months of age (this may happen even earlier), creating a need to chew to relieve gum discomfort. Some male puppies will have the physical muscle and coordination to be able to lift their legs to urinate.

What will he physically be able to do and not do between three and six months of age?

A lot. He will be able to run and play for hours, and then will crash for periods of long naps. His young bones are still forming at this age, so he can't participate safely in sustained activities, such as jogging, hiking or

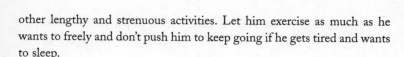

other lengthy and strenuous activities. Let him exercise as much as he wants to freely and don't push him to keep going if he gets tired and wants to sleep.

Why is socialization with other dogs and with people so important at this age for Jack Russell Terrier puppies?

Socialization is a key component in proper puppy parenting. Your young pup needs to be exposed to a wide variety of people, dogs, places and circumstances so he will grow up to be a well-adjusted dog. Proper social introductions to people, other dogs and a variety of situations should be considered important as serving nutritionally balanced meals and booking regular medical checkups with your puppy's veterinarian. Professional dog trainers and animal behaviorists recommend that puppies should meet between 100 and 200 people inside and outside your home by the age of five months.

That many people? How can I possibly accomplish this?

It is easier than you think. For instance, sit on a park bench on a Sunday afternoon for 30 minutes and you'll be amazed at the number of people who walk by or stop to pet your puppy. Even if your puppy is comfortable with the people and other pets in your house, you still need to expose your puppy to people, pets and places outside your home to make sure he is comfortable with all situations and people. This will also help him fully develop his social skills, shape his personality and hone his attitude.

What are some other easy ways to introduce my puppy to others?

Purposely introduce your puppy to anyone who comes to your door regularly, such as the meter reader, mail carrier or parcel deliverer. Have this individual give your Jack Russell pup a small food treat so that your puppy develops a positive association with this person. Encourage friends and family members familiar to your puppy to occasionally wear disguises so that your puppy becomes exposed to people wearing hats, sunglasses, beards and funky outfits. Give your puppy treats so that you pair a strange new experience with something positive. Monitor your puppy's reaction so that if he seems a little apprehensive, you can go slower and give more treats.

Why is this age often called the "juvenile period" and what can I expect?

During this juvenile period, training can be difficult because Jack Russell Terriers are physically growing so rapidly. They are full of energy and excitement and can be easily distracted. A puppy will also begin to distinguish people to the point of bonding with a particular person who offers him affection, comfort, interaction and direction. He will start to flex his independence and increase his desire to explore on his own. Within his litter and among other familiar dogs, a puppy will begin to recognize a hierarchy and where he ranks in the social standings. Puppy-to-puppy play will become more sophisticated, evolving from boxing, rolling and playful mauling to mounting for dominance, pushing and shoving to obtain possession of a prized toy. At this age, puppies quickly learn the hierarchy within their group, who has the bone and whose right it is to have that bone. They begin to develop a sophisticated body language style that they use to communicate with other dogs.

Why does it seem like my Jack Russell Terrier is acting like he forgot everything I taught him?

Recognize that your once-obedient puppy who was always by your side may temporarily forget—or conveniently choose to forget—simple learned commands such as "Come" or "Sit" or "Stay." Realize that he is about to enter into the adolescent stage, which is the canine version of the terrible twos or the teenage years.

What should my Jack Russell learn during the three- to six-month period?

Teach him house-training, basic obedience commands and the rules of the household. He will gradually grow from a toddling puppy to an adolescent, and will develop better physical coordination. His attention span will become longer, and he will learn faster as he gets older.

What kinds of things can I do with Jack Russell at this age?

You can play with him in your backyard and inside the house. Restrict his activity to these areas and other safe places (areas where other dogs have not been) until he reaches 18 weeks to avoid exposing him to potentially fatal diseases that can plague puppies. You can also take him to puppy kindergarten classes at the age of 12 weeks, if your veterinarian says it's okay, and let him play with other dogs and puppies whom you know are healthy and have been inoculated. Before the age of 18 weeks, don't take him to a park or other place where dogs frequent. He could pick up a disease in a place like this because his immune system has not yet fully developed.

How do Jack Russells develop physically between six and nine months of age?

Your Jack Russell puppy will enter a second intensive chewing phase and continue to grow in size. This is the adolescent age, so puberty and sexual maturity begin to develop in your dog. Females will experience their first estrus (heat cycle) unless spayed first. Males will develop the sexual hormone testosterone in sufficient levels to be able to mate. Unneutered males will do scent marking and may become less friendly to other male dogs, whom they view as threats or challenges.

One reason for a shift in behavior at this time is that, in wolf packs, a puppy this age would probably start looking for another pack to join or at least would detach emotionally from his mother and siblings. Since dogs inherited this developmental stage from wolves, your puppy may not see the point in paying much attention to you because he is looking for a different pack to join or different pack mates to hang out with.

What will he physically be able to do and not do during this age?

He can participate in activities like puppy agility classes, short hikes and romps at the beach. You should also let him socialize freely with other dogs. Don't jog with him until he is at least 12 months old.

What can I do during this age to reduce some of the behaviors linked to adolescence from occurring?

Book an appointment with your veterinarian to have your Jack Russell puppy spayed or neutered before nine months unless this is a dog you intend to show in conformation dog shows. (Spayed or neutered dogs are not allowed in these shows, although they can still participate in other dog sports like agility and earthdog trials.) Puppies can be safely sterilized after age eight weeks providing that they weigh at least two pounds. Reinforce your role as leader of the household pack. Rechannel your puppy's sexual energies into interactive, fun-learning games and activities. (For more information on spaying and neutering, see Chapter 4, How Healthy Are Jack Russell Terriers?)

It's important to enroll your puppy in a formal obedience training class or to continue to attend obedience school if you are already going in order to reinforce basic commands. It's vital that you train your puppy throughout the adolescent stage so he will retain his respect for your leadership. Eventually, when he grows up and out of his teenage period, he will be a better dog for it.

How do Jack Russells develop physically and mentally between 9 and 12 months of age?

A puppy will finish his physical growth by filling out his frame with muscle bulk. His body will shift its energy focus from growing taller into building muscle mass. He will start to look like an adult Jack Russell, and will lose much of his puppy awkwardness.

This time period earns the "terrible twos" nickname because a puppy often behaves like an unruly child toddler. Your puppy may show signs of stubbornness and may challenge and possibly attempt to dominate his owners and other people. He may start barking at strangers and become territorial and protective of his food bowl unless trained and socialized earlier. If your puppy is an unneutered male, he will insist on stopping every few feet on a walk to let others know his presence by leaving urine droplets. If your puppy is a female and is entering her estrus (heat cycle), she can become moody, insecure or bold. She may try to bolt out an open door in an attempt to find a male to breed with.

What can I expect from an adult Jack Russell Terrier?

Your adult will have almost as much energy as he did as a puppy, but will have lost the innocence and clumsiness of puppyhood. He will become a tenacious hunter, and will be extremely active and very smart. He will always be looking for something to do and will make his own fun if you don't provide it.

At what age is a Jack Russell considered a senior?

A Jack Russell is considered a senior after the ages of 10 through 12 years. They typically live to be 15 or older.

A senior Jack Russell is just as active as a younger Jack Russell. Unlike many other breeds, Jack Russells stay active up until the very end of their lives.

Keep in mind that older Jack Russells may develop arthritis and other health maladies that might make them a bit cranky and less likely to put up with younger dogs who want to play (assuming your pet ever liked this, since many Jack Russells simply don't like other dogs).

How can arthritis affect my Jack Russell's behavior?

He may become stiff when he walks after first getting up from a nap or coming out of his bed in the morning. After moving around, his joints should loosen up and he'll probably want to play and run almost like normal. Over time, however, the arthritis may worsen and he'll be less likely to want to run around.

Talk to your veterinarian at the first sign of arthritis in your Jack Russell. Your vet can prescribe medications that can do wonders to ease your dog's discomfort and get him running and playing again.

What are some of the other health problems that can affect my older dog's behavior?

Deafness can be a problem in older dogs, including Jack Russell Terriers. If it seems that your Jack Russell doesn't hear you when you call him, you might want to take him to the vet for an examination. If he has lost his hearing, you'll need to compensate by using vibrations to get his attention instead of vocalizations. For instance, when you approach him when he's sleeping, stomp your feet on the floor so he feels you coming and won't be startled when you touch him.

Blindness can also occur in older Jack Russells as a result of cataracts. Talk to your vet about how to treat this problem. In the event that your Jack Russell becomes totally blind, you can help him by keeping furniture and other items in the house in the same place so he learns to get around without bumping into things.

Some older dogs lose their sense of smell somewhat, and this can result in a decreased appetite. Dogs use their noses to tell them what is being served for dinner, and if your older Jack Russell can't smell his food very well, he'll be less inclined to eat it. You can remedy this problem by adding some healthy, strong-smelling food items, such as fish or garlic, to his food that will encourage him to eat. If his appetite continues to wane or drops off suddenly, call your veterinarian. Your dog may have more going on than just a weakened sense of smell.

What should I do to help my senior Jack Russell live a comfortable life?

Provide him with a warm, soft bed. Older Jack Russells are more sensitive to cold, and so a bed with a heating pad or in a warm part of the house will be most appreciated. Older Jack Russells are also more susceptible to heat, so always provide him with a cool spot to lay in, or even an air-conditioned room on very hot days.

Talk to your veterinarian about possibly changing your senior Jack Russell's diet to a prescription diet or a commercial senior dog diet. The reason for this is that older Jack Russells can develop kidney problems as a function of old age. A diet lower in protein can be easier for a senior Jack Russell to metabolize than a regular diet.

Above all, have patience with your older dog. In his later years, your older Jack Russell may have some trouble holding his urine and feces, and may have increased accidents in the house. Take him to the vet to see if there is anything that can help him control his bladder and bowels better. If not, be patient with him, and give him frequent chances to go outside to eliminate.

4

How Healthy Are Jack Russell Terriers?

How healthy are Jack Russell Terriers, in general? • What are the most common genetic health problems in Jack Russells? • How do I find a veterinarian for my Jack Russell Terrier? • What do I need to do to keep my Jack Russell in good health? • How much will it cost a year to keep my Jack Russell healthy? • Do I have to spay or neuter my Jack Russell Terrier? • Won't my Jack Russell be emotionally deprived if she isn't allowed to have at least one litter of puppies? • Are there any problems that can occur during surgery for spaying or neutering my Jack Russell? • What kind of vaccinations will my dog receive each year? • What is heartworm? • Why are fleas such a problem? • Why are ticks a problem for my dog? • How could my dog get heatstroke?

How healthy are Jack Russell Terriers, in general?

Jack Russells are hardy, healthy dogs. If you feed your dog right, give him plenty of exercise and take him to the vet at least once a year for a thorough examination, he should live a long, healthy life, assuming he is not afflicted with a genetic disease.

What do genetics have to do with a Jack Russell's health?

Genetics play a role in the health of Jack Russell Terriers and all dogs. While injuries like falls and sprains and diseases such as a cold or parasites come from the environment, a dog is born with the genes that will decide whether he has a large number of health problems. The inheritance of defects and diseases is very complex, and under certain conditions the genes for a particular disorder will not cause the dog to have the disorder. But with some genetic disorders, a dog unlucky enough to inherit the gene will certainly have a problem.

What are the most common genetic health problems in Jack Russells?

Like many other breeds, Jacks are prone to a number of genetic diseases. The most common include inherited cerebellar ataxia, patellar luxations, eye disease, Legg-Perthes disease, epilepsy, von Willebrand's disease (vWD) and deafness. Heart problems, respiratory problems, skin problems and other genetic diseases have also been found in Jack Russell Terriers.

What is inherited cerebellar ataxia?

This is a brain disease that causes puppies to lose control of their balance and muscle coordination. It occurs in the cerebellum, the part of the brain that controls balance. In dogs with the disease, certain cells in the cerebellum begin to die before their time. Puppies show exaggerated movements with their legs when walking, first apparent at between two and four months of age. They frequently fall down, and tremble when they stand still. They may also bob their heads and stand with their legs spread wide to keep from falling down. When the disease worsens, they stumble and fall, and eventually cannot get up.

Some puppies in a litter will suffer from the disease more severely than others. Some dogs who are not as badly affected can survive, but will fall down often and have trouble getting around. Eventually, these dogs may not be able to function.

Veterinarians do not know what causes these cells to die, but they know the disease is passed from carrier dogs to their offspring.

What is a "carrier dog"?

Carriers possess a recessive gene for inherited cerebellar ataxia. When two carrier dogs mate, the resulting puppies will be affected by the disease.

Can anything else cause these same symptoms?

Yes. Poisons, injuries and infections can cause cerebellar ataxia. In these cases, cells in the cerebellum also die, producing the same symptoms. Another disease in Jack Russell Terriers, called spinocerebellar ataxia, can also cause these symptoms.

How is this disease diagnosed and treated?

Vets determine whether the symptoms indicate that the puppy is affected with this disease instead of another kind of illness. The vet may also perform a spinal tap and MRI of the brain to determine whether inherited cerebellar ataxia is the culprit.

No treatment or cure exists for inherited cerebellar ataxia. Puppies affected with this disease are usually euthanized. Researchers are currently working on identifying the gene responsible for this disease. Once the gene has been identified, breeders will be able to test dogs for the disease before they breed them. It's important for owners to provide information on dogs who are victims of this disease.

How can I make sure the Jack Russell puppy I buy does not have this disease?

Since symptoms of inherited cerebellar ataxia show up in puppies only a few weeks after they are born, it is easy to tell if a puppy is suffering from this disease. Do not purchase a puppy who has trouble walking or standing.

What is patellar luxation?

This is another term for a slipped kneecap in the rear leg, caused by structural abnormalities in the patella, the flat bone at the front of the knee. The abnormalities cause the flat patella bone to shift from its normal position in the front of the knee to the side of the leg. Since the dog is not able to bend or straighten his leg normally, he seems to skip in one of his rear legs when walking or trotting. The condition may appear occasionally in some dogs, but will worsen in others until the dog ends up limping.

What is the treatment for patella luxation?

Treatment depends on the severity of the problem. Dogs with grade one severity have a minor problem that might never show up. Grade two dogs will skip on a rear leg occasionally, but don't have too many problems. Dogs with grade three severity may be in pain and show abnormal movement when they walk or trot. Grade four is the most severe. Dogs with this grade have bowed-out rear legs and are usually in pain.

Dogs with grades two through four are candidates for surgery, which can put the patella back in place. Grade two dogs have the best prognosis, while grades three and four are guarded, even with surgery.

What can I do to keep my Jack Russell from developing patella luxation?

You can't prevent this inheritable disease, but patellar luxation becomes obvious when the dog is still a puppy. You will see symptoms of the disease as the dog starts to move around more as he matures. If you see symptoms in your Jack Russell, take him to a veterinarian right away. The sooner the problem is diagnosed, the more likely surgical treatment will be effective.

The best thing you can do is to research your purchase. Look for lines with low incidence of the disease. Ask the breeder to show you the OFA certificates showing that the mother and father are free from patella luxation. If the parents are free from the disease, chances are their puppies will be too.

OFA stands for the Orthopedic Foundation for Animals. This organization registers dogs who have been evaluated for patella luxation and other bone diseases, as well as other anomalies. After receiving information from a veterinarian, the OFA issues certificates to each dog, stating whether the dog has been found to have patellar luxation or another canine bone problem.

Can a Jack Russell live with patella luxation?

Yes, especially if the condition is mild. However, dogs with severe patellar luxation can suffer considerable pain, and if this is not relieved by surgery or painkillers, your pet can have an unpleasant life.

What kinds of eye diseases do Jack Russells get?

They are most prone to juvenile cataracts, primary lens luxation, progressive retinal atrophy (PRA), distichiasis and glaucoma.

What are juvenile cataracts?

A cataract is an opaque film over the lens of the eye. In some cases, vision is not hampered at all. In others, the dog's vision can be obscured.

Juvenile cataracts show up when the dog is an older puppy, usually around the age of one year or as late as five years. This is an inherited condition, and develops when the dog inherits the tendency for this problem from both his parents.

Are juvenile cataracts different from the kind that old dogs and people get?

Yes. Cataracts in seniors are caused by a gradual thickening of the inner part of the lens of the eye. In juvenile cataracts, the outer part of the eye lens changes quickly, causing opaqueness to occur rapidly. It can take as little as six weeks for the cataract to develop.

How will I know if my Jack Russell has juvenile cataracts?

You may see white specs on the pupil of the eye, or a milky gray coating on the pupil. A veterinary ophthalmologist can diagnose the problem. In severe cases, your dog will not be able to see where he is going, and may bump into things.

What is the treatment for juvenile cataracts?

Treatment depends on the severity of the cataract. Small, partial cataracts do not obscure the dog's vision, and so as long as they don't get worse, they can be left alone. Cataracts that blur the vision have to be removed surgically. The odds are good that your Jack Russell will make a complete recovery from the surgery and get his vision back.

What can I do to make sure the puppy I buy will not develop juvenile cataracts?

Ask the breeder to show you proof that the mother and father dog have been registered with CERF. Or you can contact CERF directly to verify that both dogs have been cleared of eye disease.

CERF is the Canine Eye Registration Foundation. This organization registers dogs who have been found to be free of inherited eye disorders.

What is primary lens luxation?

This occurs when the ligaments in the eye that hold the lens in place start to deteriorate, causing the lens to become loose inside the eye. Your dog may have trouble focusing his vision. In severe cases, his eye will appear red and painful. He may even develop glaucoma or retinal detachment if the problem isn't treated.

This is another inherited condition where both parents must pass on the gene.

What kind of treatment is available for primary lens luxation?

Eye drops and medication given by mouth can help in cases where the luxation is not too severe. These medications will have to be given to the dog for the rest of his life. If the problem is severe, surgery is required.

Medication and surgery can restore your dog's sight, but only if the dog hasn't suffered severe cornea or optic nerve damage. If this occurs, surgery can eliminate pain in your dog's eye, but won't be able to bring back his sight.

How can I prevent my Jack Russell from developing primary lens luxation?

You can't prevent it, but you can limit the damage to your dog's eye by taking him to a veterinarian right away if his eyes are swollen, tearing or causing him pain. You'll know he's in pain because he will repeatedly paw at the eye. You may notice some redness or swelling, or tearing. You can also have yearly exams by a veterinary ophthalmologist.

Make sure the breeder shows you proof of CERF registration of the mother and father dogs. CERF registration confirms that both parent dogs are free from eye disease. Or you can check with CERF to verify that both dogs have been cleared of eye disease.

What is PRA?

PRA, also known as progressive retinal degeneration, is an eye disease that affects the retina. Dogs inherit the gene from both parents. The disease slowly destroys the rods and cones in the eye, which enable the dog to see. Dogs with untreated PRA eventually lose their eyesight. No known treatment or cure exists for PRA.

Jack Russells are usually adults when they begin to show signs of PRA. It begins with the dog having trouble seeing in the dark. They are afraid to go into dark places, and bump into objects when the light is dim. Eventually, they become completely blind. Their pupils become permanently dilated and an opaque film covers the eyes.

How can I be certain the puppy I buy doesn't have PRA?

Ask the breeder for a CERF certificate on both the mother and father dogs. Or you can check with CERF (Canine Eye Registration Foundation) to verify that both dogs have been cleared of PRA. During a PRA examination, a veterinarian uses an instrument called an ophthalmoscope to examine the dog's eyes after dilating the pupil with eye drops. To confirm the diagnosis, a electroretinography can be performed by a veterinary ophthalmologist. This instrument can also be used to detect PRA before the dog starts showing signs of blindness.

Since the inheritance of PRA is complex, this does not guarantee that your dog will never develop the disease.

What is distichiasis?

Distichiasis is a condition where the dog's eyelashes are placed abnormally on the eyelids. The positioning of the eyelashes causes them to rub against the dog's eye, resulting in irritation. If not treated, distichiasis can cause corneal ulcers, tearing, spasms of the eyelids and eye pain.

Dogs are born with this abnormality, and researchers believe the condition is inherited from one or both of the dog's parents.

Can distichiasis be treated?

Surgery by a veterinary ophthalmologist is the only way to correct this condition. It is usually performed using cryosurgery, where the edge of the eyelid is frozen to kill the roots of the eyelashes. If the dog is cooperative, the surgery can be performed without anesthesia.

What is glaucoma?

Glaucoma in Jack Russells is similar to the same condition in people. It is the result of pressure behind the eye, caused by fluid that has built up in the area. This fluid crushes the retina and damages the cornea and the iris. Glaucoma usually affects both eyes.

If left untreated, glaucoma makes a dog blind. Blindness can occur quickly, within 24 hours, or may take several months to completely destroy the eye.

A dog with glaucoma will be in obvious pain. He will paw at his eye and attempt to rub it. He may also act depressed and lose his appetite. To diagnose it, a veterinarian will use a special instrument to measure the intraocular pressure within the eye.

What is the treatment for glaucoma in Jack Russell Terriers?

Medications can reduce the pressure in the eye. In some cases, surgery is needed to get the eye back to normal.

What is Legg-Perthes disease?

This is a degenerative joint disease caused by an inadequate blood flow to the head of the femur bone (the thighbone; the head of the femur is the ball part of the bone that fits into the hip socket). The tissue of the femur bone dies and disintegrates. Researchers believe the illness is inherited from the dog's parents.

The disease is also known as Calve-Perthes disease, avascular necrosis, osteochondritis juvenitis and coxa plana. Usually it appears when the dog is a puppy. Most dogs exhibit the disease from three to 13 months of age; the majority develop the problem between five and eight months.

How is Legg-Perthes disease diagnosed?

Dogs suffering from Legg-Perthes limp on a back leg and have pain in the hip. One or both hip joints can be affected. To confirm a diagnosis of Legg-Perthes, the veterinarian looks for pain or crackling sounds when examining the hip area. The vet moves the leg and notes if range of motion is limited. An X ray ultimately proves the presence of the disease.

What is the treatment for Legg-Perthes disease?

Surgery to remove the diseased part of the femur bone is the most effective treatment. After surgery, the dog must rest and be placed on anti-inflammatory drugs.

Dogs who undergo surgery for this problem experience a lot less pain, and are able to move more freely. The only signs that the dog ever suffered from the disease will be a slightly shorter stride.

How can I be sure a puppy I buy does not have Legg-Perthes disease?

Researchers are currently working to identify the gene for this illness. Until then, no test is available for Jack Russells who are being bred. You must rely on the honesty of your dog's breeder to tell you if his or her dogs have ever suffered from this malady.

Why are Jack Russells prone to hereditary deafness?

The gene for deafness exists in the Jack Russell Terrier population. This gene is also present in other dog breeds, most commonly Dalmatians.

Researchers believe both parent dogs must have the gene in order to produce deaf puppies. The gene is considered recessive, meaning the parents themselves don't have to be deaf to carry the gene.

Is there a cure for hereditary deafness in Jack Russell Terriers?

No. Hearing loss is complete in one or both ears with hereditary deafness. Jack Russells with hereditary deafness can become deaf in one ear (unilaterally) or both (bilaterally). The hearing loss is complete and irreversible

How can I tell if a puppy is deaf?

When the puppy is still with his littermates, it can be difficult to tell whether it is deaf. The puppy will react to the behavior of his brothers and sisters, and will seem to be hearing you.

As the dog gets older, you will notice that he does not respond when you call him unless he can see you. He does not react to loud noises and seems startled when you come up behind him.

The only way to tell for sure is to have the breeder test the puppy's hearing by having a veterinarian do BAER testing. Also, ask the breeder whether there has been any deafness in his or her puppies in the past, and if a particular puppy's parents have been BAER tested. If the breeder has had deafness in one or both parents or in any of his or her puppies, the deafness gene exists in this breeder's dogs. In this case, the deafness gene may be present in your puppy.

BAER, which stands for Brainstem Auditory Evoked Response, is an electrodiagnostic test that confirms deafness in dogs. Only veterinarians with special equipment can perform the procedure.

Can a deaf Jack Russell live a normal life?
Yes, if the dog is deaf in only one ear. Dogs who are deaf in both ears can be a challenge to live with. They often have behavioral problems associated with their lack of hearing. They sometimes become aggressive or fearful and may be prone to biting.

What is canine epilepsy?
Similar to epilepsy in humans, canine epilepsy is a disorder of the brain resulting in seizures. The disease seems to be inherited in dogs. Trauma to the head can also cause epilepsy, as can a brain tumor. Poisoning, nutritional deficiencies, and certain metabolic diseases can also cause seizures.

What are the symptoms of epilepsy?
It depends on the type of seizure the dog has. Grand mal seizures cause the dog to fall, become unconscious and hold out his legs rigidly. The dog may even stop breathing. This is followed by paddling and chewing. The dog may also foam at the mouth and release his bladder or bowels. With milder seizures, the dog doesn't usually become unconscious, but instead twitches or jerks in one part of the body. He may also turn his head to one side.

Usually seizures do not last more than five minutes. The dog slowly recovers afterward, and may seem disoriented for a while.

What do I do if my dog is having a seizure?
Do not touch him. Observe his symptoms carefully, and then call your vet to report the incident. It's not necessary to rush your dog to an emergency clinic unless the seizure continues for more than five minutes, or if he suffers multiple seizures. Otherwise, the dog can wait to see your veterinarian the following day.

Can a seizure kill my dog?
No. Most forms of epilepsy are not life threatening. The only danger is with seizures that last more than five minutes. These types of seizures can result in brain damage.

How is epilepsy diagnosed?

Your veterinarian will make the diagnosis from the symptoms you describe. The vet may also opt to perform an electroencephalogram to verify seizure activity in the brain shortly after the dog experiences the seizure. Tests to rule out tumors and other problems will also be conducted.

What is the treatment for epilepsy?

It depends on the cause. If the epilepsy is inherited, the condition will be treated with anti-convulsant drugs that may completely or partially control the seizures. If a tumor or other problem is causing the seizures, the condition causing the seizures must be treated.

How can I be sure I am not buying a puppy with epilepsy?

What age it shows up depends on the dog and the cause of his epilepsy. The problem can begin in puppyhood, or may not show up until later in the dog's life. Ask the breeder if he or she has seen epilepsy in his or her dogs. Since no screening tests are currently available for this condition, you must go on the reputation of the breeder.

What is von Willebrand's disease (vWD)?

Von Willebrand's disease (vWD) is a blood disorder similar to hemophilia. (Humans also get this disease.) Dogs with vWD are prone to excessive bleeding. They bleed heavily when injured, when blood is taken or during surgery. Some dogs get periodic nosebleeds or bleed from the vagina or anus. Dogs with this illness do not have good clotting ability in their blood. If the dog is injured or must undergo surgery, he can bleed to death.

The gene is inherited from both parents. The disease may be evident when the dog is a puppy or may not show up until adulthood.

Is it possible to operate on a dog with vWD, such as to do a spay or neuter?

Yes, but the vet must know in advance that the dog has vWD so he or she can be prepared with blood for a transfusion.

Is there any treatment for vWD?

A medication called DDAVP is used in some cases to help dogs with vWD develop better blood-clotting ability. Unfortunately, the drug is expensive and doesn't work on all dogs.

To manage the problem, do not give medications that can thin the blood, such as aspirin, antihistamines, certain antibiotics, ibuprofen, estrogen, certain tranquilizers and theophylline. Always inform the veterinarian that your dog has vWD before the dog is treated for any condition.

How can I be sure the puppy I buy does not have vWD?

Ask the breeder for proof that both parent dogs have been tested for vWD. If both parents are affected or are carriers, their puppies will have the active form of vWD. If only one parent has the gene, then the puppy will become a carrier. If you breed that puppy, he will pass this gene to his offspring.

How do I find a veterinarian for my Jack Russell Terrier?

You can locate a veterinarian in a number of different ways. The most obvious way is to look in your local telephone directory and choose a vet near you. However, it's much better to find a veterinarian by referral than by random searching through the phone book. If you go to a vet who has been referred to you by another dog owner—or better yet, by another Jack Russell Terrier owner—you are more likely to end up with a veterinarian who is good and who knows how to treat your breed.

Why do I need to use a referral to find a good veterinarian? Aren't all veterinarians good?

Veterinarians are just like human doctors. Some are more skilled than others. By choosing a vet via referral, you are more likely to end up with a professional who is skilled at veterinarian medicine, provides good customer service and has a good bedside manner. All of these elements are important in a veterinarian, since your vet will be your partner in keeping your Jack Russell healthy throughout his life.

Start talking to other dog owners in your area. If you take your Jack Russell to the local park for a game of ball, strike up conversations with other dog owners you meet and ask them who they use for a veterinarian. You will quickly discover the name of a vet close to you who is popular with dog owners in your area.

If you have just acquired a Jack Russell Terrier puppy, ask your dog's breeder who he or she recommends for veterinary care in the area. Chances are, a vet referred by your breeder will not only be skilled at his or her profession, but will most likely have considerable experience treating Jack Russell Terriers.

What do I need to do to keep my Jack Russell in good health?

Take your dog to the veterinarian at least once a year for a checkup and annual inoculations. Spay or neuter your dog, and follow your veterinarian's advice on caring for your Jack Russell. Give your dog his regular heartworm preventative, and keep him free of fleas and ticks. Feed your Jack a quality dog food, and provide him with plenty of exercise. Keep your dog confined and on a leash so he can't get injured by a car or another dog.

What will my vet look for when he examines my Jack Russell Terrier once a year?

The vet will examine your dog's eyes, ears and mouth. He or she will also palpate (feel) your dog's internal organs. He or she will listen to your dog's lungs and heart with a stethoscope. The vet may also request a stool sample to make sure your dog is free from intestinal parasites. He or she will ask you questions about your dog's overall health.

What kind of questions will my vet ask about my Jack Russell's overall health?

The vet will ask about your dog's appetite, energy level, water intake, bowel movements and frequency of urination. The answers you provide will help the vet determine if your Jack Russell is suffering from any medical problems.

What is the vet looking for when he or she looks in my dog's eyes, ears and mouth?

The vet is checking to make sure your dog's eyes are free of eye diseases such as PRA, glaucoma or cataracts. He or she looks in your dog's ears to see if parasites such as ear mites are present. Your vet will also check your dog's mouth to see the health of your dog's teeth and gums.

What is the vet looking for when he or she palpates my dog's internal organs?

The vet is checking for any abnormalities in size and shape of your dog's liver, kidneys and abdomen. Change in size or shape of these organs can indicate internal disease.

What is the vet looking for when he or she listens to my dog's heart and lungs?

The vet is checking to make sure the lungs sound clear, and that the heart-beat is normal. This is a time when a vet might hear a heart murmur or another sound that might indicate heart disease in your dog.

What kind of parasites will the vet be looking for in a stool sample?

Roundworms, pinworms, hookworms, whipworms, ascarids, threadworms and tapeworms. All of these parasites can live in a dog's digestive system.

The vet will exam the stool under a microscope, looking for the parasite itself, or the eggs and/or larvae (offspring) of the parasite, depending on the organism.

Parasites lodge in various places, like the intestines, and feed off your dog's body. In high numbers, these parasites can make your dog anemic, give him diarrhea, cause him to lose weight and give him a generally unhealthy look. The vet will give your dog medication to kill the parasite. Your dog may have to receive more than one dose of the medication, since the drug may not work on all stages of the parasite.

How much will it cost a year to keep my Jack Russell healthy?

That depends on your particular dog. All dog owners need to spend money on an annual exam and regular inoculations. They also need to purchase heartworm preventative and flea control products. The exam and inoculations will cost you at least $100, or possibly more depending where you live. Heartworm preventive medication costs around $50 a year, and prescription flea control products another $100 to $150. Your vet may suggest performing a fecal exam to look for parasites. This will cost you an additional $20 or so. A heartworm test will also be needed. Testing is another $50. If your Jack Russell has any particular problems, you will need to spend more than these basic amounts.

What are common health care procedures likely to cost?

If your veterinarian discovers parasites in your dog's stool, your dog will need to be dewormed. This will cost you about $25 for each deworming. The number of dewormings depends on the type of parasite. Your dog may also need to have his teeth cleaned. This can cost you close to $200, especially if your Jack Russell is older and needs a complete blood panel to make certain his vital organs are functioning well and can handle the anesthetic. Also, when your Jack Russell is four to six months of age, the dog needs to be spayed or neutered. A regular neutering costs around $100 and a spay about twice that amount.

Do I have to spay or neuter my Jack Russell Terrier?

Yes, unless you bought your Jack Russell to show in conformation dog shows. If your Jack Russell is simply meant to be a companion, it's imperative that you spay or neuter your dog, for the health of your dog and for your own sanity. Female Jack Russells who are spayed live longer, healthier lives. Male Jack Russells who are neutered are happier and less likely to try to escape your yard or run away.

What exactly is spaying and neutering?

Spaying is the removal of the female reproductive organs, specifically the uterus, ovaries and fallopian tubes. In male dogs, neutering is the removal of the testicles.

Why do spayed females live longer?

Many of the ailments that can affect female dogs develop in the reproductive organs. Problems like pyometra (uterine infection) and uterine cancer are no longer an issue once a dog has been spayed. When the ovaries are removed, the release of hormones decreases, thus eliminating the likelihood of mammary cancer.

Will spaying affect the behavior of my female dog?

Yes, but in a good way. Female Jack Russells who have been spayed are more easygoing because they don't have hormones raging through their systems. They do not go into heat, and therefore will not leave blood and discharge around the house. They will be less likely to try to escape in an effort to look for a mate or become accidentally bred.

I've heard that spayed female dogs become fat and lazy. Is this true?

No, especially not in the case of Jack Russell Terriers. Your spayed Jack Russell will be as active as she was before spaying. Weight gain is the result of overeating, not of spaying. As long as you feed your dog a proper diet, you should not have a problem with her weight.

Will neutering affect the behavior of my male Jack Russell?

Yes, but the change will be positive. A neutered Jack Russell is less aggressive with other dogs, and is not preoccupied with finding females. Neutered Jack Russells are easier to train because they are less distracted by their hormones.

Won't my Jack Russell be emotionally deprived if she isn't allowed to have at least one litter of puppies?

No. Dogs don't have the same perspectives on parenthood as humans. Your female Jack Russell will have no concept of the notion that she has "missed out" on motherhood. She will still be a normal, healthy Jack Russell without having had the experience of raising a litter of puppies.

What's the harm in letting her have at least one litter?

You should not breed your Jack Russell Terrier for a number of reasons. First, your dog could experience serious complications that could result in her death. If this were to happen, not only would you lose your beloved pet, but you also might lose some or all of the puppies. The pups who remain would have to be hand fed, which is a huge job requiring care of the pups every two hours. Assuming your dog has an easy delivery and produces a healthy litter, you will find yourself with anywhere from two to five puppies to care for and place in homes. And this is expensive!

Can't I sell the puppies and make some money?

Unless you have established a reputation in the show world, it is difficult business to find good homes for Jack Russell Terrier puppies, and you may end up having to give some away or even keep some because you can't find anyone to take them. Also, by breeding your dog, you will be contributing to the unwanted pet problem in the United States. Too many dogs are homeless and euthanized each year to justify breeding more dogs just for the experience of having a litter of puppies in the house.

What is the harm in letting my male Jack Russell become a father?

While you won't have the expense and responsibility of raising a litter of puppies, you will be allowing your dog to contribute the pet surplus problem by allowing him to breed with females. Also, by neglecting to neuter him, you may find that your dog is difficult to deal with, and particularly aggressive with other males.

Are there any problems that can occur during surgery for spaying or neutering my Jack Russell?

Spaying and neutering operations are very safe. The anesthesia used today is mild, and these surgeries are extremely routine. The only exception is if complications exist before the operation. A dog with a blood disorder may require transfusions during the surgery. Male dogs who have one or two undescended testicles (testicles that are still inside the body instead of outside) require a more complicated surgery than dogs who have normal testicles.

What kind of vaccinations will my dog receive each year?

That depends on your dog's age and the preferences of your veterinarian. To avoid over-inoculating your dog, your vet may recommend only core vaccines be given to your pup. If your particular region is plagued with other ailments that can be vaccinated against, your vet may recommend one or more non-core vaccines as well.

When your Jack Russell is a young puppy, he will likely receive three sets of core inoculations over a set period of time, and may also receive one or more non-core vaccines. He may then receive yearly boosters, depending on your vet's position on this controversial topic.

What are the core vaccines he will receive as a puppy?

Between the ages of six and eight weeks, your puppy will be given his first set of core inoculations for canine distemper, canine parvovirus and canine infectious hepatitis. At six months of age, he'll receive his first rabies shot.

What are those diseases?

Canine distemper is a horrible viral disease that is highly contagious to dogs. The virus enters the dog's body through the respiratory system and then causes fever, coughing, sneezing and difficulty breathing. The virus then attacks the digestive system and causes vomiting, diarrhea, weight loss and dehydration. Many dogs die from the disease. Those who survive often have neurological problems like blindness, seizures and the inability to stand. No cure exists for canine distemper, which is why it's so important to vaccinate against this disease.

Canine parvovirus viral disease that attacks the puppy's digestive system, causing terrible diarrhea, fever and severe pain in the abdomen. The puppy can easily die of the disease, for which there is no cure, although symptoms may be treated and dehydration alleviated. This is much easier to prevent than to cure.

Infectious hepatitis virus that attacks the liver and causes inflammation to the organ. The virus causes fever, loss of appetite, vomiting, stomach pain and sometimes jaundice. This disease can kill the dog. Those who survive often have liver damage and eye problems.

Rabies is a frightening disease caused by a virus that attacks the nervous system. Dogs get rabies by being bitten by another animal who has the disease. The virus causes aggression, jaw paralysis, blindness, uncoordination and seizures. Dogs almost always die when afflicted with rabies and can be dangerous to any humans who come into contact with them.

What are the non–core vaccines my vet may recommend?

Possible non–core vaccines include inoculations for bordetella bronchiseptica (kennel cough), canine coronavirus and Lyme disease.

What are those diseases?

Parainfluenza is a virus that affects the dog's upper respiratory tract, much like the influenza virus affects humans. Dogs who contract this disease suffer from fever, coughing, sneezing and runny nose and eyes. The disease can be fatal in puppies.

Leptospirosis is a bacterial disease that invades the liver, kidneys and bladder. Bacteria enters the body through the mouth, eyes or genitals (where there are mucous membranes), causing a high fever, vomiting, bloody nose, inflammation of the inside of the eye and abdominal pain, among other symptoms. The dog may die of the disease or struggle with it for a long time before fighting it off.

Bordetella bronchiseptica, also known as kennel cough, is a bacteria spread through the air that causes dry, hacking cough. Some dogs quickly get better on their own, while others struggle with the cough for weeks. Young puppies, older dogs and dogs with respiratory problems can be severely affected by the disease.

Canine coronavirus affects the digestive system of the dog. Vomiting and diarrhea are symptoms, along with fever. Young puppies can die from this disease.

Lyme disease is a bacteria that is spread through the bite of a tick. Dogs who have been infected with Lyme disease often suffer from fever, loss of appetite, stiff joints and limping. This disease can be treated with antibiotics. Dogs who do not receive treatment can die from kidney or heart failure.

Giardia is a protozoan parasite that affects the digestive system. It causes diarrhea in most dogs, and eventually results in weakness, loss of appetite and dehydration. It can be difficult to detect in stool samples until the infection has become severe. Puppies are most severely affected by this disease, which is contracted from contaminated water or bird droppings.

What are the inoculations he will receive as an adult?

This depends on your veterinarian. There is some controversy in the veterinary community over how often a dog should be inoculated. Some veterinarians still follow the vaccine manufacturer's advice and vaccinate yearly, while others are vaccinating every one or two years. Discuss your dog's vaccination schedule with your veterinarian to find out what he or she recommends.

Are any of these diseases contagious to people?

Rabies is contagious to humans. If a person is bitten by a rabid dog, or handles an open wound on a dog who has the rabies virus present in the wound, the human can get the disease. Lyme disease also affects humans, but they must get the disease directly from a tick, and not from a dog. Humans can also contract giardia from contaminated water, but most scientists do not believe it can be directly contracted from a dog.

How do inoculations work to protect my dog?

The vaccines contain proteins of the virus and bacteria that cause the disease. When these proteins are injected into your dog's bloodstream, your dog's body creates immunities to the disease. If the dog is exposed to the actual disease, the immunities created by the vaccine work to fight off the disease.

What will happen if I decide not to have my dog vaccinated?

You stand a good chance of losing your puppy at a very young age. Most of the diseases mentioned here can be fatal to young puppies and elderly dogs. Some can also kill adult dogs, even those in good condition. The law also requires that your dog receive a rabies vaccine every three years, so you do not have a choice on this vaccine.

What is heartworm?

Heartworm is a parasite that attacks the heart muscle and can ultimately kill your dog. The disease is transmitted by mosquitoes, which inject the parasite into your dog's bloodstream when they bite your dog. The parasite then grows and develops in the dog's body and ultimately settles in the heart area. Eventually, the heart becomes so clogged with these spaghetti-like worms that it can no longer function.

Why do I have to give monthly medication for it?

Monthly heartworm medication is a preventive measure. The medication kills the heartworm in its early stages before it can migrate to the heart. Preventives also are available in daily and six-month doses. Discuss the best routine with your veterinarian.

Why does my dog need to have a yearly heartworm test?

You must verify that your dog does not have the disease. If he does have it, he will need specific treatment to kill the parasite in a way that won't damage his internal organs.

Why are fleas such a problem?

Fleas feed on the blood of dogs and other mammals. They cause itching and "hot spots," which are itchy allergic areas that your dog may scratch until they get infected and bloody. Fleas can also transmit tapeworm parasites to your dog through the bloodstream. Puppies or older dogs with severe flea infestations can suffer from anemia and may even die.

How can I tell if my dog has fleas?

You will see him scratching and biting at himself. You may also notice "flea dirt" at the base of his tail and the stomach area. These small black specs are the feces of the flea. They are easy to spot on most Jack Russell

Terriers because of the dog's white hair. To verify that you are seeing flea dirt, place these specs on a paper towel and put some water on them. If they turn red, your dog has fleas. Since fleas breed in the environment and not actually on the dog, you may even see fleas in your carpeting or on your furniture. If the infestation is bad, you may even be bitten yourself.

How did my dog get fleas?

Fleas live outdoors in the environment and wait for a warm-blooded host to come along. When they sense a mammal nearby, the flea will jump from grass or shrubs and land on the dog's body. Fleas burrow into the hair to hide themselves and get closer to the skin.

How can I keep my dog free of fleas?

Your veterinarian can provide you with once-a-month flea products to kill fleas that have bitten your dog. The fleas will die and your dog will be flea free in a matter of days.

Do I have to buy flea-control products from my vet?

No, you don't. Pet supply stores also sell once-a-month flea-control products, as well as sprays and powders. Once-a-month products are most effective, however, and are believed to be safer than sprays and powders. There is some debate over whether once-a-month products purchased from a veterinarian are more effective than those bought from a store. You can try both and decide for yourself.

Why are ticks a problem for my dog?

Ticks attach to your dog's skin and drink your dog's blood. They can spread diseases (such as Lyme disease), and in large numbers can cause anemia.

How did my dog get a tick?

Ticks live outdoors on tall grass stems and in bushes. When your dog brushes up against plant material containing ticks, the tick crawls onto the dog and burrows into the dog's hair. The tick then latches on to the dog's skin with its mouth parts.

What do I do if I see a tick on my dog?

You can grasp the head of the tick with a pair of tweezers and pull it out with one movement. If you are unsure about how to do this, take your dog to the vet. A technician can remove the tick for a lesser charge than having a vet see your dog.

How do I keep ticks off my dog?

The same once-a-month products that kill fleas also kill ticks. If you use these products regularly on your dog, ticks will die and fall off after they have latched onto your dog's skin.

Can a tick crawl off my dog and bite me?

That is unlikely. Ticks prefer to bite furred mammals. They also will not leave one host to find another. If you find yourself with a tick on your body, chances are you picked it up outdoors in a brushy area.

How could my dog get heatstroke?

Most dogs get heatstroke from being left in a hot car. Never ever leave your Jack Russell in a car in the sun, even with the windows rolled down part way. The temperature in a car can rise dramatically in a matter of minutes, and your dog can die quickly. Park in the shade if you have to leave your dog in a car, or better yet, leave him at home in his crate in a cool spot. Dogs can also get heatstroke from exerting themselves during the heat of the day. Don't encourage your Jack Russell to run around when it's hot outside. Jack Russells have a tendency to overdo it, so your dog needs you to think for him. When he's outdoors, be sure he has a bowl of fresh cool water available at all time, along with plenty of shade.

5

What Should My Jack Russell Terrier Eat?

Why is a Jack Russell's diet important? • How do I go about selecting the right commercial food for my dog? • Should I feed my adult Jack Russell Terrier once a day, twice a day or leave food out for him to nibble on all day? • How many calories of food per day should I serve my Jack Russell Terrier? • How can I tell if my Jack Russell Terrier is too chubby? • What are some healthy people foods I can give my Jack Russell as occasional treats? • What type of bowls are best for food and water? • How much water should my Jack Russell drink every day?

Why is a Jack Russell's diet important?

A good diet is crucial to keep a Jack Russell happy and healthy. Researchers have discovered that nutrition is vitally important to overall health, whether you are considering the health of a dog, a human or any animal.

Jack Russells in particular use up a lot of energy and need a quality dog food to keep their bodies running in tip-top shape.

How do I go about selecting the right commercial food for my dog?

Walk into a major pet supply store and you will find yourself pushing your shopping cart up and down rows and rows of different dog foods. The choices are many and the selection can be challenging. Do you buy dry, semi-moist or canned? Gourmet or all natural? A good starting point is to talk to your veterinarian, and then base your selection on the quality of food, not the price.

How can I find a high-quality brand of commercial dog food?

Top brands must meet food quality standards established by the Association of American Feed Control Officials (AAFCO). The first step is to look for that seal on the bag or can. The second step is to discuss with your breeder and your veterinarian about the best brands to meet your Jack Russell's needs.

What should I look for on a food label?

Protein is essential for Jack Russell Terriers. Make sure that the protein source is meat, not plant-based, because meat is easier for your dog to digest. Dogs are omnivores (meat and plant eaters). On labels, the ingredients are listed in order of quantity; the first item listed is the largest quantity. In general, high-quality brands list two or more animal protein sources within the first few ingredients, such as poultry, chicken or lamb. Low-quality brands list by-products and wheat within the first few ingredients.

Should I feed my adult Jack Russell Terrier once a day, twice a day or leave food out for him to nibble on all day?

Veterinary nutritionists recommend dividing your dog's daily portions in half and feeding once in the morning and once at night. This twice-a-day schedule maximizes your Jack Russell's metabolism and digestion of the food. Stick with a regular schedule because if you feed once a day and then twice a day, you can throw off the feeding schedule and cause some health and behavior problems in your dog. Research has revealed that dogs who free feed—meaning they have access to a full bowl of food all day—tend to become overweight.

How many times a day should I feed my puppy?

By his first birthday, your young Jack Russell Terrier is a fast-growing puppy who will multiply his birth weight eight times. A Jack Russell pup needs twice the calories of an adult, but be careful not to overfeed. Up to age three months, your puppy benefits most by being fed four times a day. Remember that your puppy has an itty-bitty stomach and needs to be fed several times a day to be able to digest the food properly. Between three and six months of age, your puppy should be fed three times a day. By six months of age, your puppy is ready for twice-a-day feedings.

How many calories of food per day should I serve my Jack Russell Terrier?

In general, veterinary nutritionists recommend the following guideline for optimal canine calorie intake. (Take into account your Jack Russell's age, activity level and health.) In general, an adult Jack Russell Terrier should consume from 500 to 700 calories of food per day (that's about 1½ cups of dry food). They require more calories than other dogs of their size because of their supercharged natures.

What should I serve my Jack Russell Terrier: dry food, semi-moist or canned food?

Always check with your veterinarian first to help select the best commercial diet that meets your Jack Russell's specific age, activity level and overall health. That said, the pros of dry foods are that the hard pieces of kibble can help prevent major buildup of tartar and plaque on your dog's teeth. Plus, dry food costs less per serving than canned food, and is more convenient to serve. The main drawback is that your fussy eating Jack Russell may snub the dry food. Also, dry food cannot be stored for very long without losing its nutritional value. If your dog's dry food is more than a month old, it will have lost much of its freshness.

Semi-moist dog food delivers great taste and is easy to pack on trips. The downside is that semi-moist food usually contains a high amount of sugar and its texture can cling to your dog's teeth.

The advantages of canned food are palatability and the fact that 75 percent of the canned food is moisture to ensure your dog is getting enough liquid in his daily diet. The disadvantage of canned food is that it doesn't provide fiber substance and may contain sugar. It can also be messy to serve, and harder to take with you when you travel.

How can I tell if my Jack Russell Terrier is too chubby?

Rely on the rib test. First, place your thumbs on your Jack Russell's backbone and spread your fingers across his rib cage. You should be able to feel your dog's ribs, but they should not be protruding out. Then stand over your dog as he is standing and look at his profile. A Jack Russell at a healthy weight will have an hourglass shape with a clearly defined abdomen slightly tucked up behind his rib cage. In other words, you should be able to see his waist.

My Jack Russell Terrier really loves to eat. How can I prevent him from becoming a beggar when we eat meals?

The best advice is to never succumb to those begging eyes in the first place. Ignore your puppy's pleas for table scraps and he will eventually get the message and stop begging. If you want to give people food to your puppy, wait until after you've finished your meal and then put a small piece in his food bowl. You can also feed your puppy in his crate so that it can serve as his own personal dining room.

My young Jack Russell Terrier pup is teething and wants to chew everything in sight. Is it safe to give him a real bone to gnaw on?

Unfortunately, real bones—especially chicken, turkey, pork and fish bones—can create a slew of problems for dogs. These bones can splinter and cause intestinal obstructions. They can also harbor parasites and cause stomach upsets. Opt for a safer alternative for your must-chew puppy by giving him nylon bones or rawhide chew strips.

What safe foods can I offer my young Jack Russell Terrier to ease his need to chew?

Here's a safe, quick and easy homemade recipe ideal for Jack Russells. Take an ice cube tray and pour water into each of the cube holders about two-thirds full. Fill the rest with beef or chicken gravy. Store this special canine ice cube tray in the freezer until you want to serve a meaty treat. The icy cube will satisfy your Jack Russell's need to chew and ease his sore gums as well.

What are some healthy people foods I can give my Jack Russell as occasional treats?

Depending on your Jack Russell's individual palate, most seem to enjoy performing tricks and obedience commands for air-popped popcorn, apple slices, broccoli and raw carrots. All of these treats are low in calories. They are also nutritious. Be sure to give them only in moderation, however, or your Jack Russell will end up with a stomachache and/or diarrhea.

I love onions. Can I feed them to my dog?

Onions contain large amounts of sulfur, which can destroy red blood cells and cause severe anemic reactions in some dogs. So why take the chance? In small quantities, onions may cause no problems, but in some Jack Russells, onions can trigger vomiting, diarrhea, constipation and internal bleeding.

My Jack Russell Terrier loves to nose around the kitchen when I'm baking chocolate chip cookies. Is it okay to treat him to a cookie?

No. Chocolate may be a sweet treat for you, but for your Jack Russell, it can be downright deadly. The reason? Chocolate contains theobromine, a chemical that can cause life-threatening diarrhea in dogs. The most dangerous type of chocolate is baking chocolate because it contains nearly nine times more of this dangerous chemical than milk chocolate. As little as three ounces of baking chocolate can kill a dog the size of a Jack Russell Terrier.

Another reason not to give him that cookie is that it is more than likely loaded with fat and sugar. Neither of these items is good for your dog.

How can I make an herbal broth for my Jack Russell Terrier?

Give your dog a healthy herbal broth to pour over his dry kibble sometimes. The easiest way is to use two herbal tea bags or four teaspoons of dried herbs and allow them to simmer or steep in one quart of boiling water for 15 to 20 minutes. Remove the tea bags or strain out the dried herb and let the broth cool. Pour ¼ to ½ cup of this herbal broth over your Jack Russell's dry food. You can also add some of this herbal liquid to the water bowl. Store the rest of the herbal broth in a container with a lid in the refrigerator to keep it fresh.

What type of bowls are best for food and water?

The best choices are stainless steel bowls with nonskid features. These bowls are dishwasher safe and durable. Be careful of ceramic pet dishes because they are breakable, and make sure that they are double-glazed to prevent harmful bacteria growth. Also, steer clear of plastic bowls that can be chewed on and harbor bacteria.

My Jack Russell Terrier likes to drink out of the toilet bowl. Is that bad?

Yes. Although this behavior seems to be etched into the genes of every dog on the planet, it's not a good thing. Even after flushing, the water in the toilet contains bacteria and germs that can make your dog sick. Get in the habit of keeping the lid on the toilet or shutting the bathroom door to block access.

How much water should my Jack Russell drink every day?

On average, your Jack Russell requires about 15 to 20 ounces of water per day. The water source can come from the faucet as well as the water from canned food. Make sure your Jack Russell has access to an unlimited supply of fresh water every day. Each morning, clean and fill water bowls with fresh, filtered water two or three times. You can add some ice cubes if your Jack Russell likes to crunch on cubes.

How can I tell if my Jack Russell Terrier is dehydrated?

To check to see if your Jack Russell is dehydrated, lift the skin on your dog's back near his neck. Release it and see how quickly the skin snaps back. It should be firm and return to shape within a few seconds. If the skin does not return to shape or takes a long time, these are signs that your dog is dehydrated and you need to have him examined by your veterinarian right away.

6

How Much Exercise Does a Jack Russell Terrier Need?

🐾 I've been considering a Jack Russell in part because of their size. Is it true they don't need much exercise because they're fairly small? • How much walking do adult Jack Russells need? • I live in an apartment and work all day. Is that going to be a problem? • What kind of leash and collar are best for walking? • Can I hire a dog walker? • Are dog parks good places to take Jack Russells? • Can I let him run off lead in an unfenced area? • I have a fenced yard. Do I still need to walk him? • Are there ways to exercise a Jack Russell in the house? • Is it ever too hot or too cold to exercise a Jack Russell outside? • Is agility good exercise? • How do I know if my dog isn't getting enough exercise? 🐾

I've been considering a Jack Russell in part because of their size. Is it true they don't need much exercise because they're fairly small?

Jack Russells need a lot of exercise. True, they take a lot more steps to cross a room than a big dog does. The difference is a big dog gets tired of crossing the room, and a Jack Russell never gets tired of doing anything. Jacks are the Energizer Bunnies of the dog world; they keep going and going and going. Remember what Jack Russells were bred to do: go out in the field and keep up with the hounds and seek out vermin. This takes a lot of energy for a fairly small dog.

What about a puppy?

Very young puppies have lots of energy spurts and lots of down time. So if you bring home a baby Jack when he's 8 or 10 weeks old, he'll probably be pretty easy to manage for a while. But the older he gets, the longer he can go, and by the time he's 6 or 8 months of age, you'll be wondering what happened to that sweet little tyke you used to have. That's when a lot of people give up on them. He'll remain extremely active for several years, and then taper off somewhat when he's 4 or 5, or maybe 10 years old—it varies from one Jack to another.

How much walking do adult Jack Russells need?

A lot. If you work, plan on waking up an hour earlier every day and getting in a 45-minute walk before you get ready to leave. And when you get home, plan on another, longer walk. Your dog will still be raring to go after an hour, but then he'll still be raring to go after two hours, so any time after an hour you're entitled to turn back toward home.

That seems like a lot of walking. Is there some way to speed up his exercise sessions?

Keep in mind that if you're already trying to figure out ways to get through exercise sessions faster, this may be a bad sign that your heart is not into having a dog who needs a lot of activity. But if you want to accelerate your exercise sessions so you can spend time doing other activities with your dog, then there are several ways you can do this. You can cover the same amount of ground you would on a walk, but just do it faster. Jogging is a great way to get both of you in shape. Even if you don't like jogging, you should try to get in a few sprints in any walk. Ball playing is good too—or agility. Jacks can fly!

I live in an apartment and work all day. Is that going to be a problem?

Unless somebody's home with him, it will almost certainly be a problem. Even a well-exercised Jack Russell is too inquisitive and active to spend the day alone in a confined area. He can get into too much trouble if you let him have the run of the place, and he will be too frustrated if you keep him crated for long periods. If you are home with him you can break up his day and have several play sessions, which would help a lot.

What if I walk him in the morning and evening?

That's a good start. The problem is most people start running late in the morning, and that morning walk ends up being a quick potty trip outside and back. Then at night it may get dark early or the weather gets bad, so that walk gets abbreviated. Pretty soon they end up having a dog who's getting almost no exercise. If you commit to making your dog depend on you for exercise, then you have to do it no matter how late you are, how bad the weather is or how many other more enticing engagements you have.

What kind of leash and collar are best for walking?

For a collar, the main requirement is that it must not be able to slip over his head. Many buckle collars can do this, so a slip (called choke) collar or better, a martingale collar, may be better if you're walking near traffic. Neither of these is to be used when you aren't around, as they can choke your dog. Whatever collar you use should have a license tag attached. For a leash, use a sturdy leather or nylon leash, not chain. Harnesses are also an option. You can also get an extendable leash. These are handy for giving your dog some extra freedom as long as you don't let him interfere with other people or dogs or allow him to run in front of cars or bikes.

Can I hire a dog walker?

That depends on your dog and your finances. Dog walkers can be expensive, so you may want to check how much it would cost for you to have your dog walked every day. Most professional dog walkers walk lots of dogs at once, so your dog has to be able to get along with other dogs. That makes it especially important for you to socialize your Jack with other dogs, because some Jacks aren't good with other dogs.

What about paying a neighborhood kid to exercise him?

Again, that depends. If you're gone all day hiring a responsible dog-savvy child to come and interact with your dog can be a good idea. A lot of young people would welcome the chance to be paid just to play with a dog. But they have to know that it's a big responsibility. They must be diligent about never letting the dog get loose, and they need to know what to do in case of emergency. It's not a good idea to allow a child to take the dog on long walks or to take the dog to other places, even dog parks, where the dog could run off lead. And you must take into consideration not only the dog's safety, but the child's. They should never be in an isolated location, and should always have an adult on call.

Is doggy day care a good way for my dog to get his exercise during the day?

Doggy day care is a good way to make sure your dog gets both mental and physical exercise every day, especially if you work. It will add significantly to your dog-owning expense, but it may save you money in the long run that you would otherwise spend on home repairs. Your dog's enjoyment of it will depend on how well he gets along with strange people and other dogs. If you plan to go this route, you should get him used to visiting daycare from an early age. Just as with a child, consider staying with him the first few times as he gets used to it. Make sure the facility is safe and that they do more than just keep the dogs in cages. They should have exercises and games for your dog to partake in.

Are dog parks good places to take Jack Russells?

Dog parks are fenced areas where dogs can run off leash and mingle with other dogs. Some are simply large enclosures, and others have trails and obstacle courses. A dog park can be a good place to take your Jack as long as he is good with other dogs. You can meet other owners there and have a good time while your dogs play together. Many dog parks have separate large dog and small dog areas. Jack Russells are difficult to sort, however, since they are small in size but big in attitude. If you let them mingle with large dogs, they may take on more than they can handle, but if you put them with the small dogs, they may scare less assertive dogs. If there are too many dogs running together, a single yelp could make all the dogs chase and perhaps even attack the yelping dog. But even if your dog is well behaved, the other dogs may not be. Always keep an eye on your dog and be ready to step in should trouble arise.

Can I let him run off lead in an unfenced area?

Not if you don't want to hunt for him. You really need a securely fenced area before you can let your Jack off lead. Remember how these dogs like to hunt. Your Jack could catch the scent or sight of a wild animal and decide to follow it, maybe into traffic or even underground! In fact, some Jacks just pop down any hole in the ground they come across, and they've been known to be lost underground for days! No dog should be allowed to roam loose in the neighborhood, but this is even more true for Jack Russells than other breeds. They are not homebodies and they tend to wander off in search of adventure without thinking of how they might find their way back home.

I have a yard, but it isn't fenced. What about putting him in a dog pen or on a long line so he can get outdoors?

Neither of these will give your dog much exercise. True, he can run in circles in a pen, but that's not mentally stimulating and if he's allowed to do it continuously, it could even lead to some behavior problems. Chaining him is even worse. If you want to tie him to you or beside you as you work in the garden, that's fine, but he can't ever be tied when by himself. It's too dangerous and he won't get any exercise.

I have a fenced yard. Do I still need to walk him?

A fenced yard will be a huge help, but it doesn't take the place of you. For your dog, half the point of a walk is spending time with you. A walk also lets your Jack exercise his mind by sniffing all the interesting smells, seeing new scenery and possibly meeting new people and dogs. A yard is a good place for your Jack to entertain himself, but eventually even the most interesting yard gets old. When that happens some Jacks find the most intriguing challenge is finding a way to escape from the yard. Bored Jacks excel at digging and clawing and squeezing their way to freedom.

Are there ways to exercise a Jack Russell in the house?

Only somewhat. You're never going to get your dog physically exhausted with house games, but you can exercise his brain, and that can be just as tiring as strenuous physical activity. In fact, a fit Jack Russell is one who gets challenging mental and physical exercise every day. So one thing you can do is to train your Jack Russell. You don't have to limit yourself to the standard obedience training exercises; after all, this is for fun. You can teach tricks and maybe even shape him into a future movie star. You can test his treat and ball-catching skills, teach him to bark on cue or show him how to deliver messages from one person to another. You can even play with balloons or soap bubbles. You can hide treats and toys around the house and let your dog search for them, either by memory or by scent. If you don't mind a few broken lamps, you can play fetch inside. If he doesn't run up and down stairs too carelessly, you can send him up and down after the ball until he gets tired. You can dance with your dog too! But even with all these activities, he's still a dog who needs to play outdoors, and he won't be satisfied until he's had some invigorating outdoor activity as well.

Are laser lights a good exercise toy?

That's a loaded question! Jack Russells made laser lights—those pointing devices that shoot out a pinpoint beam of red light—popular as a dog toy. Many dogs love chasing the light around the room. This can be a really fun game for a rainy night. The problem is that a few dogs love this game a little too much. They've learned that they can search for the light and it often blinks back on. So even after you've quit the game and left the room, they continue searching. Some Jack Russells become obsessed with finding it, so obsessed that they look everywhere for it, dig up sofa cushions, stare at spots on the floor, chase shadows and in extreme cases they even quit playing other games, eating, sleeping or being an affectionate companion. These dogs need drug and behavior therapy in order to recover, as they seem to suffer from obsessive-compulsive behavior. Jack Russells develop this problem in response to laser lights more than any other breed. Laser lights may be OK for occasional use, and many Jacks never have a problem with them, but at the first sign of obsessive behavior the light should be thrown in the trash.

Is it ever too hot or too cold to exercise a Jack Russell outside?

Jack Russells can do well in chilly weather as long as they're moving around. They enjoy playing in the snow but eventually you may need to bring them inside to warm up. They're not suited to Arctic temperatures and must be shielded from such extremes.

As with any breed, strenuous exercise in the heat can lead to death. Dogs can't cool themselves by sweating, so most of their cooling depends on panting.

How would I know if my dog was overheating?

A dog who is panting heavily and has a swollen, dry-looking tongue is certainly overheating. In later stages he may have convulsions. An overheated dog needs to be cooled rapidly, usually by wetting him. That's one reason it's essential to have lots of water around if you exercise your dog in hot weather. But really, you need to keep your dog inside when it's hot out.

How do I exercise my dog in the summer if he can't exert himself in hot weather?

Owning a Jack Russell in a warm climate can be challenging because it's hard to find a cool enough time to exercise him outdoors. You can play a lot of indoor games during the day and then take your outdoor walks late at night or early in the morning. Carry a canteen of cool water with you. Wet down his body as much as possible.

I live where it snows a lot. I know they aren't sled dogs, but are there other ways to exercise Jack Russells in the snow?

They may not be sled dogs, but Jacks are always up to a new challenge, so who knows? They might just be an entertaining sled dog team. You'll have better luck with a sport that requires less teamwork, though. Skijoring is a fun activity in which your dog helps pull you along on skis. You'll need to teach him some commands to go right, left, faster, slower, and stop. You can attach from one to three dogs for extra dog power, as long as they all go in the same direction. Dogs love to skijor and it burns off energy quickly. As with every sport, you need to work up gradually, and don't expect to just stand there while your dog does all the work.

Is agility good exercise?

Agility is the fastest-growing dog sport in the country, and Jack Russells are one of the best dogs at it. You may have seen dogs in competition racing from obstacle to obstacle, jumping over high jumps and through tire jumps, climbing steep A-frames, balancing across raised walkways and moving teeter totters, running through tunnels and weaving around poles. You can bet these dogs are burning up calories! Not all dogs, however, approach an agility obstacle course at breakneck speed. One advantage of using agility to condition your dog is that many naturally tend to start slow and build up to more taxing levels of performance. Still, that doesn't mean you can ignore basic conditioning. If your dog isn't used to jumping, he can hurt himself or be sore for a couple of days afterward, which could set him back in his training and exercise. Start with a few low jumps and adjust each day, building up gradually.

How do I know if my dog isn't getting enough exercise?

Your first clue might be your demolished home. That Jack Russell energy has to go somewhere, and, if he has no other outlet, he will chew your furniture, rip down your curtains and dig up your carpet. He may bark incessantly. He may run in circles or just jump in place. He may direct his frustration at his own body, chewing and licking until he creates a sore. He may be disobedient and seem unfocused. He may gain weight and become obese.

I feel like I can't exercise my Jack any more than I do, but he's driving me crazy. What else can I do?

You probably don't want to hear now that you were warned. But you were. Underestimating the Jack Russell's energy level and overestimating the ability to meet them is the number one reason Jacks are given up to shelters and rescue. But you love your Jack and just want him to calm down. First, don't exile him to the garage or a pen in the yard or a chain out back. This will only make him worse. You can provide him with a safe quiet-time place, perhaps a crate or exercise pen that is still around the family, where he can spend up to a couple of hours at a time. Get him started on a regimented exercise routine, one where he knows what time of day he will be walked and what time he will not be. Stick to it. Give him an hour in the morning and an hour in the evening. Have well-defined play times. You can do this by having special toys you use during these play sessions and then put away when you're through. Devote 10 minutes in the morning and 10 minutes in the evening to training, longer if you're teaching tricks that are lots of fun. You can adjust this schedule if you're home during the day. Consider hiring somebody to walk or play with him in the middle of the day if you're not home. The goal is to tire both his body and his mind. Take him to obedience or agility classes as many times a week as you can manage. Even therapy dog classes would be of help. Consider getting another, larger dog for him to play with (probably not another Jack Russell Terrier, though). Consult a certified animal behavior counselor for one-on-one therapy. If you can't do this, you can always wait for several years and he might calm down on his own. But if your only other choice is to put him in a pen by himself and forget him, he would be better off placed with a Jack Russell Terrier rescue group.

7

What's Involved in Training a Jack Russell Terrier?

 How easy or hard are Jack Russells to train? • What kinds of things can I train my Jack Russell to do? • How much time will it take to train my Jack Russell to be a well-behaved pet? • Do I have to go to a class to train my Jack Russell? • How soon can I start training my Jack Russell puppy? • How do I know if I need a private trainer to come to my home to train my dog? • How can I house-train my Jack Russell Terrier? • Isn't a crate just a cage? Isn't it cruel to keep a dog in a cage? • Where should I keep my dog's crate? • How hard is it to house-train a Jack Russell Terrier? • How can I train my Jack Russell puppy to behave inside the house? • How can I keep my Jack Russell from doing damage in my backyard? • Can my Jack Russell Terrier live in my backyard? • Why can't I let my Jack Russell bite my hands? He is only playing.

How easy or hard are Jack Russells to train?

They are *hard* to train. Like all terriers, they are independent and sometimes stubborn, and call for patience and creativity when training. The good news is that Jack Russells are very intelligent, and if you can motivate your dog to learn (food is a good way), then your dog will learn quickly.

Why are Jack Russells independent?

Having an independent nature is part of being a terrier. And Jack Russells are all terrier! Terriers were originally bred to work independently of their masters, and needed to be able to think on their own and make their own decisions. When a Jack Russell was out in the field hunting vermin, he couldn't look to his master for guidance about where the rat was hiding, where the rat might run and how to get to the rat once it went underground. The dog had to figure all this out by himself. This means the Jack Russell had to learn to think on this own, to figure out problems without guidance, and to basically function very independently. Even though many Jack Russells today live simply as companions, they still retain that same personality as their working ancestors. Consequently, most Jack Russells have their own ideas about how to do things, and this makes them tougher to train.

Why does this independent streak make them harder to train?

Because they don't have the natural instinct to look to a human for guidance, as would a Golden Retriever or an Irish Setter. Breeds such as those two, as well as Labs and Cocker Spaniels and other bird hunting breeds, were developed to hunt on the commands of their handlers. Bird hunters who work with dogs control the movements of their dogs very specifically, telling them when to retrieve the bird, when to drop it, and so forth. Jack Russells, on the other hand, were left to their own devices when the breed was developing. They did not acquire the need to listen to a handler, and instead were encouraged to hunt on their own and often did. This personality trait can be a real challenge when you are trying to tell them what to do while you are training them.

Is there anything particular or special about a Jack Russell that I need to remember when I'm training my dog?

Because Jack Russells are independent and easily bored, too much repetition is a sure way to bore them. They are not naturally inclined to listen to your every word, so you need to convince them that it's worth their while to obey you. Do this by keeping training sessions short and fun, and always use positive methods rather than punishment. It's important to be patient, and don't give up. Positive training is when you reward the dog for doing what you have asked, and avoid punishing him for not doing it. Jack Russells respond well to these methods because it motivates them to learn. Once they figure out there is something in it for them, they become much more agreeable to training.

Why are Jack Russells so easily bored during training?

They are very intelligent dogs who lose interest during training sessions because they often just don't see the point. Unlike breeds that were developed to pay close attention to a handler, they don't have the inclination to listen. They also don't get as much joy out of pleasing you as does a breed that was created to work closely with humans. Most Jack Russells would rather be off playing somewhere or hunting for mice instead of being taught to sit, come, etc. Frankly, they just don't see the point to it. Also, they learn quickly and get bored doing something over and over again.

What kinds of things can I train my Jack Russell to do?

You can teach him to compete in dog sports. Agility, flyball and earthdog trials are favorite sports among Jack Russell Terriers because they involve running fast and doing stuff that Jack Russells love to do, like climbing, chasing balls and running underground.

How can I get involved with these events?

You and your dog will need formal training for each of these sports. This means you'll need to sign up for classes to learn how the sport works and how you can teach your Jack Russell the ins and outs. The American Kennel Club sanctions agility and earthdog trials, and provides information on how to get involved with these events. Flyball is not an AKC event, but is sanctioned by the North American Flyball Association. The organization provides information on how to get involved with this sport. (For information on these organizations, see How Can I Learn More? in the resources section.)

How much time will it take to train my Jack Russell to be a well-behaved pet?

You will need to work hard at training your puppy the first year of his life, all day, every day. This means constantly teaching him how to behave, and reinforcing all commands. When your Jack Russell is a puppy, he is most open and eager to learn, so now is the time to show him the ropes. Specific training sessions — when you teach him to sit, stay, etc. — should be once or twice a day, for no more than 10 minutes per day. You should attend regular obedience classes (called "puppy kindergarten") for at least eight weeks (usually one class per week), and then continue his training at home or take other more advanced training classes to help you make your dog a better pet.

Is a puppy too young for training?

A puppy eight weeks or older is old enough to start training. In fact, the younger the dog, the easier he is to train. If you think of a puppy like a child, it makes sense. Whether you are talking about a dog or a human, youngsters like to learn. Their brains are still developing, and this is the time when they are most open to new experiences.

How can I train my dog 24/7?

By always being aware of what he is doing and what he should be learning. Watch him all the time, and know what he is up to. One of the most important aspects of training is teaching the right habits. If you don't let your Jack Russell learn bad habits like chewing the furniture, but instead get him in the habit of chewing on a toy, this is what he will learn. In order to have control over your puppy, keep him on a leash and let him drag it around. When you need to stop him from doing something, you can just reach for the leash. When you call him to come to you, reinforce it by grabbing the leash and making him come if he doesn't do it after the first request. Remember to keep him crated when you can't supervise him so he doesn't learn those bad habits. Think of your Jack Russell as you would a toddler. Keep his whereabouts and behavior in your mind at all times. You need to keep a constant watch on him and tell him when he is doing right (with praise, treats or a toy), or when he is doing wrong (a redirection of his behavior to something else.)

Do I have to go to a class to train my Jack Russell?

It's a good idea to take your Jack Russell to obedience class rather than just trying to train him on your own. The reason is that obedience class gives your puppy the chance to socialize with other dogs. Obedience class also provides a structured environment where you can train your dog, instruction for you on how to train your dog and the expertise of a trainer who can assist you if you have problems with your pet. Also, Jack Russells are easily distracted by activities in their environment, and obedience class is a good place to teach your dog to pay attention to you regardless of what is going on around him.

Why do I need to socialize my Jack Russell with other dogs?

Jack Russells have a natural tendency to be aggressive with other dogs. This is the terrier in them. If your Jack Russell learns to play with other dogs as a puppy, chances are he'll grow up with more tolerance for other dogs and will be less likely to pick fights as an adult.

What happens to my Jack Russell's behavior if I don't have the time to train him regularly, especially when he is a puppy?

You will end up with an unruly, badly behaved dog who will be unpleasant to live with, and is likely to end up in an animal shelter because you won't be able to deal with him. When Jack Russells are bad, they are very bad. Don't learn this the hard way by not training your dog.

Why will he become unruly? Lots of dogs don't get training and they are fine.

All dogs need training to learn to behave properly, and Jack Russells more so because of their busy, assertive natures. Jack Russell find a way to expend their energy in unacceptable ways if you don't teach them how to properly behave. You'll be horrified to find out how they can learn to amuse themselves if they don't have rules to fall back on.

How soon can I start training my Jack Russell puppy?

You should start the moment your puppy comes to live with you. Puppies are ready, eager and willing to learn, whether it's house-training, basic obedience commands like "come" and "sit" or the rules of the house (no chewing on the furniture!). Even if your puppy is only eight weeks old and has the attention span of a gnat, you can still teach him. Things like "sit" and "come" can be learned by very young puppies. It will be more difficult to teach him not to chew on the furniture because at this age, puppies are very single-minded. That's where the chew toys and the crate come in. Redirect your puppy's chewing to something appropriate, and put him in his crate if you can't watch him.

Keep training sessions short, fun and consistent. Give lots of praise and treats, and don't be afraid to backtrack in the training if necessary. Above all, be patient! Jack Russells can be very trying on the nerves, so take a deep breath and remind yourself that training a terrier is always a challenge.

Can an adult Jack Russell Terrier be trained?

Yes, but it's always easier to start with a puppy. An untrained adult Jack Russell already has bad habits established that you will have to break. It will take much more effort to deprogram the stuff the adult dog has already learned, and then teach him the right behaviors, than it would be to teach a puppy right the first time. This is not to say that adult Jack Russell Terriers can't learn like some of the Jack Russells you've seen on movies and TV. The dog who plays Eddie on *Frasier* was an adult when he was taught all the tricks and behaviors he does on the show.

How do I know if I need a private trainer to come to my home to train my dog?

Professional trainers are only needed in situations where a Jack Russell has a behavioral problem, such as barking excessively, acting aggressively or being destructive. If you can't deal with your Jack Russell's behavior, you can call a private trainer who knows terriers and specifically Jack Russells. It's good to get a reference from a veterinarian, from another dog owner or from a dog club. You may also be able to find a certified animal behaviorist in your area to help you with your dog. These individuals are usually veterinarians and have extensive training in dog behavior. They tend to charge more than professional trainers, but have the advantage of being able to prescribe medications if your dog needs them.

How can I house-train my Jack Russell Terrier?

The best way to train a Jack Russell to eliminate outdoors is to use a crate. By keeping your puppy in a crate when you can't supervise him and taking him outdoors frequently to go to the bathroom (every couple of hours), you'll help him develop the habit of going outdoors to potty. Be sure to praise him verbally immediately after he does his business outdoors. Tell him he is the most wonderful dog in the world because he relieved himself outside.

What is a crate and how do I use it?

A crate is a container for shipping or confining animals, and comes in different styles. Plastic, airline-approved crates are most commonly used for dogs, although folding wire metal crates are also popular. Your crate becomes your dog's "den" and a place where he will not eliminate. If you crate train your dog, he will learn to love his crate and think of it as a safe haven.

Why won't my dog eliminate in the crate?

It's against his instincts to go to the bathroom in his own bed. If he views the crate as his bed, he will make every effort to hold it until you get him outside.

Isn't a crate just a cage? Isn't it cruel to keep a dog in a cage?

A crate is not cruel if you use it properly. You should use a crate to confine your Jack Russell Terrier when you can't supervise him and when you are traveling with your dog in a car or on a plane. If you do not leave your Jack Russell confined for too long, it is not cruel to keep your dog in a crate. He will think of it as his bed, and so will you.

How long can I keep my Jack Russell in a crate?

Not more than four hours at a time. If he gets plenty of exercise both before and after he goes in the crate, he will most likely sleep during his confinement.

Won't my Jack Russell hate being in the crate?

Not if you gradually get him used to being confined, if you don't abuse the crate by keeping your dog in it for too long. Make his crate a happy place by feeding him in it and putting toys in it that he can chew on or play with while you are gone.

How do I gradually get him used to the crate?

You can feed him in it and keep the door closed for longer and longer times until he is used to being inside with the door shut. Placing a toy filled with peanut butter or spreadable cheese inside the crate also helps the dog have a good association with being confined. While you are out running errands or working in the house, he'll be busy trying to get the food out of that toy and won't give a hoot about being confined. Eventually, he'll realize that being in the crate means he gets food, as well as a private place to rest.

Can an adult Jack Russell learn to use a crate?

It's harder to get an adult Jack Russell used to a crate than it is a puppy, but you can do it by feeding the dog inside the crate first with the door open and then eventually closed for short periods of time. Gradually increase the time the door is closed. Give him goodies when he's in the crate so he comes to associate it with something pleasant.

Where should I keep my dog's crate?

The best place for your dog's crate is in your bedroom. Keeping your Jack Russell's crate in your bedroom gives him more time with you, and encourages the bond between you. It will also keep your puppy from feeling lonely at night. Having him with you also gives you the opportunity to hear your puppy whimper in the middle of the night if he has to go to the bathroom. On the other hand, don't let him out every time he cries or he'll quickly learn that crying is the way out. If you take him out to go to the bathroom, put him right back in the crate afterwards. Only let him out after he's been quiet for at least five minutes.

Should I put a dog bed inside the crate?

Not if your dog is a young puppy because he will likely chew up the bed. Start with a thick layer of newspaper, and when your pup has outgrown the teething stage, you can try a towel or a blanket. Keep a close eye on your Jack Russell to make sure he's not chewing up the bedding. If he swallows pieces of it, his intestines may become blocked. If chews up his bedding, you'll need to remove it and go back to newspaper.

Can my puppy stay in the crate through the night without having to go to the bathroom?

If your Jack Russell is eight weeks old or older, he should be able to make it through the night without having to go to the bathroom, provided you haven't given him food and water about two hours before putting him in at night. Give him his last meal several hours before bedtime.

Should I put water in my puppy's crate at night?

Your puppy can go without water during the night while he is sleeping. It's not a good idea to put a water source in the crate, since he may need to go to the bathroom in the middle of the night if you do this. (If you don't mind being woken up in the middle of the night for a potty break, then feel free to give him water.) The other possibility is that he might knock into it and spill water all over himself during the night. It's best to keep water out of the crate at night.

How hard is it to house-train a Jack Russell Terrier?

It's not easy. The breed's independent nature does not lend itself to house-training. Jack Russells have their own ideas about things and are just as likely to think the living room rug is as good a place to pee as the back-yard. You'll need a lot of patience to teach your puppy not to go to the bathroom in the house.

Are there any tricks to house-training a puppy using a crate?

Yes. Remember not to give your puppy food less than two hours before you crate him. Also, remove his water about an hour before putting him in his crate if he is going to stay in it for more than a couple of hours. Take him out of the crate only when you can watch him indoors. You don't want him to develop the habit of going to the bathroom in the house.

How long will it take to house-train my Jack Russell Terrier?

Jack Russells are notoriously difficult to house-train, so it may be a good six months before your dog is reliable indoors without going to the bathroom. Expect to have mistakes, but remember that it's important to set your Jack Russell up for success by giving him many opportunities to go outside to potty.

How can I train my Jack Russell puppy to behave inside the house?

Your first obligation is to puppy proof your home to make sure it's safe and free of potential problem spots. Then, be sure to watch him at all times when he is running lose. If you can't watch him, put him in his crate or a puppy exercise pen. If you see him chewing on something he shouldn't, give him something appropriate to chew on (like a chew toy) to get him in the right habit.

How do I puppy-proof my home?

Cover or remove anything your Jack Russell may be tempted to chew on. Keep in mind that he'll want to chew on just about everything. This includes furniture legs, electrical cords, houseplants, shoes, clothes and whatever else might be within reach. You can also use deterrent sprays like Bitter Apple, available at pet supply stores, to help discourage him from chewing. Spraying it on an item gives that item a bad taste. (Be aware that not all Jack Russells are deterred by Bitter Apple spray because of their toughness and tenacity.)

How do I keep my Jack Russell puppy from chewing on electrical or telephone cords?

The best way to do this is to keep a close eye on him at all times. Know where he is and what he is doing. Also, move these items out of reach where your puppy can't get to them. If your puppy chews through an electrical cord, he can be electrocuted and possibly start a fire in your house, so it's important that you keep him from doing this. You should also unplug the cords as much as you can to help prevent him chewing through a live wire.

How can I keep my Jack Russell from doing damage in my backyard?

Move potted plants, garden tools and decorative wooden items out of your puppy's reach to avoid having damage to these items. Protect your flower beds with surrounding chicken wire, and bury it into the ground at least a foot because Jack Russell are compulsive diggers. Keep a close eye on your puppy to see what he's up to. If he starts fixating on a particular item and is determined to chew or otherwise harm it, you'll need to get that item out of harm's reach. Give him something else to chew on instead.

What can I do to keep my Jack Russell puppy safe in the backyard?

You need to puppy-proof your yard to make sure your dog doesn't get into anything. Puppies will try to eat snail poison and other toxic chemicals and will chew on toxic plants. The ways they can get into trouble have no end.

Besides ingesting pesticides and other poisons and eating toxic plants, puppies can be killed by predators such as coyotes and birds of prey. Be especially careful during the hours of dawn or dusk when predators do most of their hunting. Don't leave your puppy outside unsupervised.

Can I train my Jack Russell to stay in my backyard?

No, you can't. Jack Russells love to roam, and you will need a tall fence (at least five feet high) that is well buried in the ground to keep your Jack Russell on your property. Remember that Jacks are great jumpers and climbers, so don't keep anything piled up along your fence that will serve as a stairway for your tenacious terrier!

Can my Jack Russell Terrier live in my backyard?

No! Jack Russells need both an indoor and an outdoor life. If you try to relegate your Jack to outdoors only, your dog will become lonely and unhappy. The result will be a destructive dog who chews and digs, barks incessantly and tries to escape from the yard.

Can I get two Jack Russells and let them keep each other company outside?

That's not a good idea for a few reasons. For one thing, Jack Russells need human companionship. You can't substitute another dog for human inter-action. Second, two Jack Russells can get into twice as much trouble as one. Just because they are together doesn't mean they won't get bored and start looking for things to destroy or ways to escape. Last, terriers often fight with one another. Leaving two Jack Russells alone unsupervised can result in one or both of the dogs being severely injured or even killed.

Why can't I let my Jack Russell bite my hands? He is only playing.

Not only does it hurt to have sharp dog teeth on your skin, but it's also a bad habit for your Jack Russell to get into. Biting should be prohibited, no matter what the context.

My Jack Russell bites and pulls at my clothes. Is this OK?

Never! Your Jack Russell must learn to respect you. When he does this, walk away and ignore him. He needs to learn that this is unacceptable behavior. Your Jack must know you are the head of the household, or he'll become a tyrant.

If he bites your hands while playing, say *"No bite!"* right away, stop the game and walk away. It's normal for puppies to be mouthy, but you must teach your Jack Russell from a young age that teeth are not to make con-tact with human flesh under any circumstances.

8

How Do I Groom My Jack Russell Terrier?

 What's involved in grooming a Jack Russell Terrier? • What's involved in grooming a rough or broken-coated Jack Russell Terrier? • Will I ever be able to convince my very active Jack Russell to sit still for grooming? • How often should I groom my Jack Russell Terrier? • How much do Jack Russells shed? • How often should I bathe my Jack Russell Terrier? • What do I use to clean my Jack Russell's ears? • What's involved with trimming a Jack Russell's nails? • What do I use to brush my Jack Russell's teeth?

What's involved in grooming a Jack Russell Terrier?

This depends on the kind of coat the dog has. Jack Russells can have smooth coats, or rough or broken coats. Each of these kinds of coats is handled differently. If you have a smooth-coated dog, you should hand strip (pluck) your dog's coat or have a professional groomer do it. If you have a rough or broken-coated Jack Russell, you can easily do this yourself.

You also need to clean your dog's ears and trim his toenails as part of his grooming routine. Tooth brushing is also part of grooming and should be done every day. A regular bath is also a must if your Jack is to smell and look his best. Stinky Jack Russells are not as huggable as nice clean ones.

What is hand stripping?

Hand stripping, also called plucking, is the removing of excessive hair by hand using something called a stripping knife. Stripping knives come in different blade sizes, each for a different part of the dog's body. A coarse knife is for the main part of the body, a medium knife for the dog's shoulders and neck, and a fine knife for the ears and rest of the head. You will need three different stripping knives to hand strip your Jack Russell Terrier. Most pet supply stores carry hand stripping tools for terriers. Or you can purchase them through a dog supply catalog or over the Internet. Stripping knives run about $15 to $30, depending on the size and quality of the knife.

How does hand stripping work?

You hold the stripping knife in your right hand and put a few of the dog's hairs between the knife blade and your thumb. You then give a sharp tug on the hair. This pulls the dead hair out of the coat, and it ends up on the knife.

Does hand stripping hurt the dog?

Some people say it does, while others say no. This has long been a minor controversy in the terrier world. Dogs who have never been hand stripped are clearly uncomfortable with the process and need to get used to it before they stand completely still for this. Some people liken it to tweezing human eyebrows. It's really uncomfortable in the beginning, but after you've done it for a while, the discomfort is barely noticeable.

I'm nervous about doing this by myself and ruining his coat. How can I learn to do it properly before I start grooming my dog?

You can ask your Jack's breeder to show you how to hand strip. Any Jack Russell breeder worth his or her salt knows how to hand strip a terrier. You can also take your dog to a professional groomer to have him hand stripped and save yourself the worry. You will have to pay for the service, but it may be worth your while if you are really uncomfortable with the idea or if you just don't have time.

Will it be hard to find a professional groomer who knows how to groom a Jack Russell Terrier?

No. Most dog groomers are familiar with this procedure because many terrier breeds require hand stripping as part of their grooming process. Just be sure to ask the groomer in advance if he or she has had much experience with this technique. If your Jack Russell has never been hand stripped, be sure to tell this to the groomer so he or she knows to go easy on your dog the first time out.

What's involved in grooming a rough or broken-coated Jack Russell Terrier?

A Jack Russell with this kind of coat is much easier to groom than a smooth-coated Jack. All you have to do is brush the dog with a slicker brush to get rid of the loose hair that has built up in his coat. Then clip around the dog's body with electric clippers to shorten the hair on his body.

What is a slicker brush and where can I get one?

A slicker brush has a handle with wire pins that protrude from the head of the brush. You can buy one at any pet supply store. They come in different sizes, so be sure to get one that is on the smaller size to fit your Jack Russell Terrier. These brushes are great because they pick up loose hair from the dog's coat and trap the hair in the pins. You can easily pull the hair out of the brush when you are finished and discard it.

Is it hard to use electric clippers to trim a Jack Russell's hair?

No. In fact, clippers are pretty easy to use once you get the hang of it. Go light at first, since it's better to take off less hair than too much. "Float" the clippers around your dog's body to trim off hair that is sticking up. No one likes an unkempt Jack Russell Terrier! Most clippers come with a guide that tells you how to use them. Follow this guide and you should be all right.

You can buy clippers at pet supply stores. A decent pair of clippers and blades can run you anywhere from $30 to $50. Keep in mind that you'll save money if you do the clipping yourself rather than paying a professional groomer to do it.

Will I ever be able to convince my very active Jack Russell to sit still for grooming?

Yes, if you make it fun for your dog. Jack Russells love a good game, and they love yummy treats. Reward your dog every few minutes for standing still so he learns that grooming time means a game of ball or a favorite treat. Using this reward technique to make grooming a pleasant experience for your Jack will be time consuming and requires patience on your part, but it is well worth the trouble in the long run. Nothing is more aggravating than trying to hand strip or brush a squirming, uncooperative dog. You won't be able to strong-arm your tenacious terrier into cooperating, so it's best to try to win him over into thinking that grooming is a good thing.

How often should I groom my Jack Russell Terrier?

This depends on your particular dog and how fast his coat grows out. You should only have to hand strip or clip him every few months. You should brush him weekly, though, to help loosen dirt from his coat and reduce shedding. He'll need his toenails trimmed every six weeks or so, depending on how fast they grow. Many dogs wear down their toenails just by running around on concrete or asphalt. If you are lucky, your Jack Russell is one of these dogs and won't need frequent toenail clipping.

What happens if I decide not to groom my Jack Russell Terrier?

He will begin to look pretty unkempt and ratty. No rule says you have to strip his coat or brush him, but if you want him to look like the handsome Jack Russells you see in books, magazines and on TV, you'll need to make this effort. Also, if you don't groom him regularly, he will start to shed more and more, to the point that you have more loose dog hair in your house than you thought possible. If you don't bathe him regularly, he will start to smell bad and will also start to get itchy from accumulated dirt and dead skin.

How much do Jack Russells shed?

A lot. And because most of their hair is white, it is particularly noticeable around the house, on your clothes and on the furniture. If you don't stay on top of brushing, you will soon start finding Jack Russell hair in your food, on top of your dining room table and all over your clothing.

Is there anything I can do to reduce my Jack Russell's shedding?

Yes. Brush him frequently. The more often you brush him, the more often his loose hair will end up in your brush instead of in your house.

How often should I bathe my Jack Russell Terrier?

Bathe him as often as he needs it, probably at least once a month. Your nose will tell you when he is ready for a bath. Active dogs like Jack Russells often get into messy situations and need to be washed pretty frequently. The good news is that their coats are designed to repel dirt, and so mud tends to fall right off them after it dries.

What should I use to wash him? Can I use people shampoo?

It's a good idea to use a shampoo that is designed specifically for dogs. The reason for this is not just to line the pockets of dog shampoo manufacturers—dog shampoo is actually different than human shampoo. Dogs have a different skin pH than do humans, and so dog shampoo is less likely to irritate your dog's skin than your own shampoo.

What do I use to clean my Jack Russell's ears?

Using a cotton ball moistened with water, or a commercially made ear wipe, clean out the inside of your Jack Russell's ear flaps. Don't go too deep. You just want to get rid of the dirt you can see when you look at your dog's head straight on.

Why do I need to do this?

Clean ears are nicer to look at, and are also less irritating to your dog. Also, it gives you a chance to examine his ears to make sure they smell okay and aren't full of ear mites or riddled with infection.

How will I know if my Jack Russell has ear mites or an ear infection?

The inside of one or both ears will be caked with dark, waxy build up. They may also have a foul odor. If you see either one of these problems, take your Jack Russell to a veterinarian for an exam and medication.

What's involved with trimming a Jack Russell's nails?

You will need a pair of nail clippers made especially for trimming a dog's nails. You hold the dog's paws out one at a time and trim each toenail individually.

You can buy clippers at a pet supply store. You'll see different types. Some are guillotine style while others are more like human toenail clippers. The one you choose is a matter of preference. Ask your dog's breeder, if you have one, to recommend the type he or she prefers.

Why is it important to trim my dog's nails?

If your Jack Russell's toenails get too long, your dog will have trouble walking. Think about how you feel when your toenails are too long. While your Jack won't be wearing shoes that will pinch him, he will have to walk with long, curving nails pressing against the ground. This will be uncomfortable for him. It may even affect the way he walks or may damage his feet.

Will my Jack Russell tolerate this procedure?

If you start when he's a puppy, he will be better behaved about it than if you just grab him one day when he's full grown and start trimming away. Jack Russells aren't thrilled about having their feet touched to begin with, so it's a good idea to get your puppy used to having his paws handled.

If you got him as an adult, you can still teach him to tolerate having his nails trimmed, but it will take a lot more patience and cajoling. Use treats and toys to help him associate toenail trimming with something positive.

I'm nervous about doing this. Can I have a vet or groomer do it?

Yes, you can. You'll need to pay to have it done, so you may want to watch the procedure being performed by one of these professionals and then try it at home yourself. The worst thing that can happen is you will cut into the quick and cause a bit of pain and bleeding. You can stop the bleeding with styptic powder, the kind men use when they cut themselves shaving.

The downside of this is that if you hurt your Jack by cutting too close to the quick, he may not be very cooperative next time you try to trim his toenails.

What do I use to brush my Jack Russell's teeth?

A doggy toothbrush and doggy toothpaste will do the trick. Pet supply stores carry all three of these items. You may even find toothpaste in different dog-friendly flavors, such as chicken, beef or peanut butter. You can also use a piece of gauze wrapped around your finger with some doggy toothpaste on it, or else a rubber finger brush with bristles on the end.

A canine toothbrush looks very much like a human toothbrush, although the handle is longer and has a different curve than toothbrushes made for people. A rubber finger brush is a cap that fits over your index finger. Small bristles at the end of the cap work in the same way as a toothbrush to massage the dog's gums and teeth and remove plaque.

Studies have shown that a toothbrush is more effective in removing plaque on a dog's teeth than a finger brush. On the other hand, some people find a finger brush to be easier to use than a toothbrush.

9

Where Should I Get My Jack Russell Terrier?

 Are Jack Russell Terriers hard to find? • What about the Internet? • I see some Jack Russells with long legs and some with short legs. Why? • Which makes a better pet, a male or a female? • Where should I get my Jack Russell Terrier? • What is a rescue group? • What is a responsible breeder? • How much do Jack Russell Terriers cost? • What is meant by "pet quality" and "show quality"? • How do I find a responsible breeder? • What should I expect in terms of a guarantee? • The breeder I contacted wants me to spay or neuter the dog. Why? • How can I buy a Jack Russell Terrier I can show? • I have seen two clubs for the Jack Russell Terrier. Are they different? • Do papers mean a dog is better? • I want a Jack Russell Terrier puppy right now. Can I get one quickly from a breeder? • When can I see the puppies? • What should I look for in a puppy? • How can I tell if the puppies are healthy? • What do I need to have on hand before I bring home my Jack Russell? • I can't wait for everyone to meet my new dog! Any advice?

Are Jack Russell Terriers hard to find?

Not these days. With their media exposure, Jack Russells have become very popular. Unfortunately, this means that a lot of people are breeding them just to cash in on their popularity. This makes finding a good Jack Russell Terrier more of a challenge.

What about the Internet?

The Internet is a good place to browse and visit the sites of various breeders. It's not always a good place to shop for puppies, though, especially if you go to one of the multi-breed puppy selling sites (more than two breeds). People who sell more than one breed are not focusing exclusively on breeding good Jack Russell Terriers, and may be breeding dogs indiscriminately. The best way to use the Internet is to find several Jack Russell Terrier sites and then look for links to pages of serious breeders who breed only Jack Russells or perhaps one other breed in addition. Remember it is very easy to present a glowing but sometimes misleading picture of perfection over the Internet.

Don't make a decision based on the Internet alone. Expand your search to phone calls, letters and, if possible, personal visits.

What about Internet discussion groups?

Joining an Internet discussion group devoted to Jack Russells is a good way to get to know various breeders, and for them to get to know you. First you'll have to find a good list to join. The typical general pet-oriented group will not be good enough to meet your needs because breeders may not be present on these lists. If you're interested in showing, also consider joining a list devoted to showing all different breeds. Such a list may have members who can help direct your search further. Specialized lists also exist for interests in agility, obedience, tracking, therapy and earthdog.

I see some Jack Russells with long legs and some with short legs. Why?

Leg length reflects the varied history of the breed. The Jack Russell Terrier was developed in England as a hunting dog. Anglican Parson John Russell is credited with first developing the breed in the early 1800s. Derived from Fox Terriers, Jack Russells were initially used to run with foxhounds and go to ground after the foxes. They eventually became sought after by farmers and hunters for their skills as earthdogs (dogs who could hunt underground vermin by digging). Longer-legged Jacks reflect the original type favored by the parson for foxhunting. Shorter-legged Jacks found favor with hunters more concerned with badger digs and other types of hunting that were done mostly underground. Jack Russells were first imported to the United States after World War II, and were treasured as hunting dogs. The breed has grown in popularity ever since, but the difference in leg length has remained a source of great controversy.

What is an English Jack Russell Terrier?

The English Jack Russell Terrier is a subtype of the breed that has short legs. They should be between 8 and 12 inches tall at the withers, and have short legs in proportion to their height. The English Jack Russell Terrier Alliance was established to seek recognition for these short-legged terriers.

Which makes a better pet, a male or a female?

They both make equally charming and mischievous companions. Some breeders describe males as more people oriented and females as more hunting oriented, but the differences are not obvious. Plus, each dog is an individual, and it's often hard to generalize. Females come into estrus twice a year unless you have them spayed. This means they have blood flow from the vagina that can be messy. They will try to escape in the effort to find a mate. Males are always ready to sow their oats unless you have them neutered. They have a tendency to roam in search of females and are often more aggressive with other dogs than neutered males. Spaying and neutering tends to make both sexes easier to live with.

Where should I get my Jack Russell Terrier?

The best place is from a Jack Russell Terrier rescue group or from a responsible Jack Russell Terrier breeder.

Can I find these groups or breeders in the newspaper?

Sometimes a rescue group will place an ad, and sometimes a responsible breeder might, but more often the ads you find in the newspaper come from backyard breeders.

What are backyard breeders?

These are usually people who happen to have a Jack Russell Terrier or two and decide to breed them either to make money, or for the fun of it, or because their neighbor said they wanted a puppy. Unfortunately they don't usually know much about dogs or Jack Russells and because of that they don't screen their breeding stock for health problems or provide optimal prenatal or puppy care. It's also unlikely they'll guarantee their pups.

What is a rescue group?

A Jack Russell Terrier rescue group is a private organization dedicated to taking in Jack Russell Terriers from animal shelters or from individuals who can no longer keep them and placing them in good homes where they are wanted.

Why would I want a dog from a rescue group? Aren't they sort of like damaged merchandise?

Offering a homeless dog a place in your heart is a gratifying experience. True, some rescue Jacks have had bad experiences that will require extra patience and understanding on your part, but most rescue Jacks are simply normal Jack Russell Terriers who had the misfortune of ending up in a family who could not cope with normal Jack Russell behavior or had personal problems of their own. A good rescue group will be able to tell you which Jacks have special needs.

If rescue groups don't advertise in the paper, how will I find them?

You can look on the Internet or contact the American Kennel Club or one of the national Jack Russell Terrier clubs for a list of Jack Russell Terrier rescue groups around the country. If possible, contact a group that is located near your home. (For contact information, see the resources section, How Can I Learn More?)

Will the rescue group ask me questions?

The rescue contact wants to make sure you will be able to handle a Jack Russell Terrier. After all, the reason most of the dogs are in rescue is that they were first owned by people who were not prepared for the Jack Russell way of life. The questions may include:

- Have you ever had a dog before?
- What happened to your previous dogs?
- Have you ever had a Jack Russell Terrier before?
- Why do you want a Jack Russell Terrier?
- Do you have any children? If so, what are their ages?
- Do you own a home or rent?
- Do you have a fenced yard?
- Do you have any other pets?
- Do you work out of the home during the day or at night?
- Would the dog be left alone while you are at work?
- How much time can you devote to exercising, training or playing with your dog each day?

The rescue contact may also set up a home visit to make sure your house and yard are suitable for a Jack Russell Terrier. They are looking to see if you have a securely fenced yard, and that you have presented your situation truthfully in your application. For instance, if you said you had no children and the rescue contact discovered five small neighbor kids playing in your backyard, they might decide you don't have the right lifestyle for a Jack Russell.

What if the rescue contact thinks I should not have a Jack Russell?

They will politely tell you so and possibly suggest another breed based on your experience with dogs and your lifestyle. Please don't be offended. Rescue contacts want to place their dogs, but placing them in a situation that is likely to fail again is even worse for the dog than staying put in a foster home a while longer. It's easier to fall in love with the Jack Russell Terrier idea than it is to live with one in real life.

What do Jack Russell Terrier rescue groups consider a good match?

The ideal Jack Russell Terrier person is someone who is very active and who can spend a lot of time with the dog. It helps if the person is not a stickler for perfect white rugs and immaculate yards. Rescue groups prefer someone who lives in a house, and who either owns the house or has permission from the landlord to keep a dog. The house should have a fenced yard, and the person should have owned a dog before. Children should be at least six years of age. Since other pets can be harassed or even killed by a Jack Russell, the rescue contact will want to make sure you are aware of this.

Will I have to pay for the dog I adopt from the rescue group?

Yes. Most rescue groups charge an adoption fee to help offset the costs of rescuing a Jack Russell. Typical rescue expenses include routine veterinary care, spaying or neutering, food, transportation, plus occasional large veterinary bills. Besides, just because he's a rescue doesn't mean he's worthless—far from it! People tend to value things, often including dogs, more when they pay for them.

Can I get a puppy from a Jack Russell Terrier rescue group?

Probably not. Most of the dogs who come from rescue groups are adult dogs between the ages of one and three years, in need of homes. That's the typical time it takes for a person who has bought a puppy to realize they're overwhelmed. Puppies only occasionally end up in Jack Russell rescue, usually because they arrived with their dam, who was rescued with the litter or was pregnant when she was rescued.

Why would I want to get an adult Jack Russell Terrier instead of a puppy?

Adults are often easier to handle, assuming they don't have behavioral problems. Adult Jack Russells have already gone past the puppy stage, and are often house-trained, and have outgrown teething. Some adult dogs have already been obedience trained.

With an adult dog, you will know what you are getting right away, unlike a puppy, who will have to grow up before you get the full picture. You will be able to see the dog's temperament if the dog is an adult, as opposed to waiting for a puppy to mature to discover his personality. You will also be saving the life of a Jack Russell Terrier who needs a home.

What kind of behavioral problems could a rescue dog have?

Abandoned Jack Russells can come with many kinds of typical dog problems, including separation anxiety, inability to get along with other dogs or a dislike of children. (For more information on these problems, see Chapter 2.) Excessive activity and barking are probably the most common complaint of former owners, but that's pretty usual behavior for the breed.

The foster "parent" should have explained these to you beforehand so you don't take a dog with problems without knowing it. However, some problems don't show up until the dog is placed in its permanent home. The rescue group will give you advice and put you in touch with a trainer who can help you deal with your dog's problems.

What if things don't work out with the dog once I adopt him?

You can return the Jack Russell to the rescue group to be placed in a different home.

What is a responsible breeder?

Responsible breeders are those who breed dogs as a hobby, not for profit. They compete with their dogs in some venue and breed with the intent of improving the Jack Russell Terrier breed. They screen their dogs for health problems when this type of testing is available, and guarantee the health of their puppies. They socialize their puppies at a young age and provide advice and guidance for those who purchase their pups. They take responsibility for the dogs they breed, and will take a dog back at any stage of its life if the owner can no longer keep it.

Why should I buy a Jack Russell Terrier from a breeder when I can buy one at my local pet shop?

You will get a better dog from a breeder. Most of the puppies sold in pet shops come from puppy mills, facilities that breed dogs in large numbers strictly for profit. These puppies are not socialized at a young age, live in inhumane conditions and often have health problems, some of which don't show up until the pup is older. They can also be harder to house-train because they have spent so much time in a cage.

Isn't it cheaper to buy a puppy from a pet shop than from a breeder?

No. Ironically, puppies sold in pet shops usually cost much more than puppies purchased from a responsible breeder. Yet the responsible breeder has many times more money invested in the dogs.

How much do Jack Russell Terriers cost?

Expect to pay anywhere from $350 to $600 for a pet-quality Jack Russell Terrier, and significantly more for a show-quality dog. (For more information on the cost of buying and owning a Jack Russell, see Chapter 10.) Remember that a responsible breeder has a lot invested in your puppy. The breeding stock cost more to begin with. She spent money and time training and competing with the dogs to prove their merit, having health screening tests, breeding the female to the best rather than the closest male Jack Russell and providing her with prenatal testing and care. She may have stayed home from work to care for the pups, and has applied years of research into providing the best care and socialization for your potential puppy. She will be available to you for the next 15 years whenever you have a question or problem.

In contrast, the backyard breeder has bought the cheapest dog available, bred it to the closest male Jack Russell available and thinks it's a major financial investment if the pups have their first shots and are wormed. And the puppy mill has invested even less than that in the puppies who are available at a pet store.

What is meant by "pet quality" and "show quality"?

Pet quality, also called companion quality, refers to a dog who has the major attributes of his breed in appearance, but may have some flaw noticeable to breed purists that would prevent him from being a successful show dog. A pet-quality puppy should have good temperament and good health.

Show quality refers to a dog who meets the breed's standard of the ideal closely enough so that he can compete in dog shows with a reasonable expectation of finishing a championship. Jack Russell Terriers also have hunting quality, which refers to a dog who comes from hunting or earthdog stock and can reasonably be expected to be successful in those venues. For anything but pet quality you will need to seek out a breeder who has had success in those areas.

How do I find a responsible breeder?

Start with the American Kennel Club, the United Kennel Club or one of the Jack Russell Terrier clubs. You can also look in dog magazines or Jack Russell Terrier magazines. If you go through a breeder affiliated with a Jack Russell club, you are doing business with a breeder who has agreed to uphold the ethics set forth by the club. To ensure that a breeder is responsible, you will need to ask certain questions.

What are the questions I should ask to find out if a breeder is responsible?

- Are you involved with a Jack Russell Terrier breed club?
- Do you raise your puppies indoors?
- Do you evaluate the temperament of your puppies?
- Will you take the dog back if I can't keep him for some reason?
- If I buy a puppy from you, can I call you with questions or about problems I might have with the dog?
- Have the puppy's parents been screened for Jack Russell health disorders, such as deafness, lens luxation and patellar luxation?
- Have the puppy's parents earned any titles in conformation, obedience, agility or earthdog competitions?
- Can I meet the mother of the puppies?
- Can you provide references and telephone numbers of other people who have purchased puppies from you?
- Do you provide a written contract and a health guarantee with the purchase of a puppy?

The answer to all these questions should be "yes."

Will the breeder ask me any questions?

Yes. A responsible breeder will screen you carefully before agreeing to sell you one of his or her puppies. The breeder will want to know about the place you live, whether you own or rent, if you have ever had dogs before, how much you know about Jack Russell Terriers and whether you have children or other pets. He or she will also ask if you have a fenced-in yard and how much time you have to spend with a dog. Don't be offended by these questions. The breeder wants to know if you can provide a good home for a Jack Russell Terrier. You gain nothing by trying to mislead the breeder into thinking you are better prepared than you really are. Nobody—least of all the dog—wins from that ruse.

What should I expect in terms of a guarantee?

Dogs are living creatures and as such can't be warranted like a mechanical object. A breeder can give you a guarantee against certain defects, however. These might include specific diseases, perhaps with a time limit. Perhaps the dog will be guaranteed to pass a hearing test at four months of age or to be free of patellar luxation at a year. You will probably have to provide veterinary certification and will also probably have to have your dog neutered or spayed.

I always read in newspaper ads the phrase "shots and wormed." Isn't that a guarantee the pups are in good health?

That's just the beginning of health care. Your pup should have his first shots by the time you bring him home. He may or may not need to be wormed. Your breeder and veterinarian can advise what's best for your particular dog. By the way, most responsible breeders don't consider "shots and wormed" to be a big enough deal to mention in an ad. Only backyard breeders who don't know what other positive things to say about their pups usually bother to mention it.

Are there any health tests that can be performed on puppies?

Your purchase should be contingent on your taking your new pup to a veterinarian for a health exam within a couple of days of getting him. Your veterinarian may find a problem that could affect your pup's future, and you should have the option of returning him for a full refund if that's the case. The veterinarian will examine him for skin conditions and parasites, listen to his heart and look at his teeth, eyes and ears. Because some Jack Russells, particularly ones with a lot of white on them, can be deaf, your veterinarian may test your dog's hearing. (For more information about this test, see Chapter 4.)

The breeder I contacted wants me to spay or neuter the dog. Why?

To reduce the overpopulation of dogs in general, and to reduce the chance that a descendant might end up in rescue. Responsible breeders who sell Jack Russells as pets are obligated to make sure their puppies don't contribute to these problems. If you are buying the puppy as a pet, you should spay or neuter the dog, both for ethical reasons and for the dog's health. (For more information on spaying or neutering, see Chapter 4.)

How can I buy a Jack Russell Terrier I can show?

You have to buy a show dog from a breeder involved in conformation showing. It's not easy to find a Jack Russell Terrier breeder willing to sell a show-quality puppy to a stranger. (For more information about show-quality puppies, see Chapter 10.)

Why is it hard to find a breeder who will sell me a show-quality Jack Russell?

Show-quality pups aren't born that often, and breeders usually want to keep for themselves. They also worry that your interest in showing may be fleeting, and their show prospect will never be shown or will be bred carelessly. However, the breeder may be willing to have a co-ownership agreement with you.

What is co-ownership? Is it a good idea?

You and the breeder own the dog together, but the dog lives with you. The breeder might show the dog for you, and the dog lives at your home when not being shown. (For more information about co-ownership, see Chapter 10.)

It depends on the individuals involved. Get everything in writing, think of every contingency and don't agree to a situation that you don't like. Be aware that your Jack Russell will be gone much of the time at dog shows instead of staying home with you. If the dog is a female, the breeder will want to breed the dog. The birthing process can be risky for the dog. Also, you may be asked to care for the puppies (a lot of work) or else have the dog stay with the breeder after the puppies are born.

I have seen two clubs for the Jack Russell Terrier. Are they different?

Yes. The Jack Russell Terrier is represented by two breed clubs in the United States: The Jack Russell Terrier Club of America (JRTCA) and the Parson Russell Terrier Association of America (PRTAA).

Why does the Jack Russell Terrier have two clubs?

Jack Russell breeders don't agree on certain aspects of how the Jack Russell should look or how they should be registered. The Jack Russell Terrier Club of America was the only club until it split into two groups in 1987. The newer club is the Parson Russell Terrier Association of America (PRTAA), which sought AKC recognition. The JRTCA preferred to remain independent of the AKC. Each club promotes a different type of Jack Russell, with size being the primary difference. The JRTCA advocates a 12- to 15-inch-tall Jack Russell, while the PRTAA promotes a dog ranging from 10 to 15 inches.

Does the American Kennel Club register Jack Russell Terriers?

Yes. In 1996, the American Kennel Club recognized the Jack Russell Terrier as a distinct breed of dog. As of 2003, AKC-registered Jack Russell Terriers became known as Parson Russell Terriers.

Do papers mean a dog is better?

Registration with a reputable organization simply means that your dog comes from registered stock that can be traced for several generations. If you wish to compete in conformation or to breed your dog with the expectation of registering the offspring, registration is necessary. But registration is no guarantee of quality. It is not necessary in order for a dog to be a superior companion. (For more information about this, see Chapter 10.)

What sort of registration papers should I expect?

You should receive a pedigree with your puppy, along with registration papers to the applicable registry. For AKC registration, the breeder will have already registered the litter. You or the breeder must then choose a name for your pup and send in his individual registration form before he's registered. JRTCA registration is a little more difficult. You must wait until the pup is over a year old and then submit a pedigree, veterinary certificate saying the dog is clear of hereditary defects and color photographs of the dog. He must be between 12 and 15 inches tall at the withers (shoulders). (For more information about registering your dog with the JRTCA, see Chapter 10.)

Do I get to name the pup or does the breeder?

This varies from breeder to breeder. It's customary for the breeder to require that the breeder's kennel name be included as part of his registered name. It usually goes first. Some breeders use different themes for each litter, so people can quickly identify littermates. That means your pup's name may have to start with a certain letter, include a certain word or be related to a certain group of items. Of course, you can call your pup whatever you want; it need not reflect his registered name.

What is a registered kennel name?

This is a kennel name that has been registered with the AKC, UKC or JRTCA by the breeder. Only registered kennel names can appear in a dog's official name.

I want a Jack Russell Terrier puppy right now. Can I get one quickly from a breeder?

Probably not. Most responsible breeders wait until they have enough prospective buyers before they breed a litter. Once you find a breeder you like you may have to wait before she is ready to breed a litter. If a litter is expected, you will have to wait at least eight weeks before the puppies are available to go to new homes.

What can I do if no puppies are available?

You can look for another breeder (although you will probably run into the same situation) or just wait those few months before a litter is born and the pups are ready to go to homes. During that time you can learn more about the breed. Breeders prefer potential buyers who show this kind of commitment.

What if I don't want to wait?

Waiting is the price you pay for getting your puppy from a good breeder. It's worth the sacrifice. If you buy impulsively from a pet shop, you will spend more money and end up with a Jack Russell who may have health or behavioral problems. You can also consider adopting a dog from Jack Russell rescue group if you want to get a dog soon. You won't get a puppy but you should be able to get an adult dog right away.

When can I see the puppies?

Many breeders are very protective of their puppies. Because some potentially fatal diseases can be carried on your hands or shoes, they may not allow you to visit the pups until they are several weeks old. Keep in mind that the mother dog will look her very worst while she is nursing. She may have a scraggly coat and large teats, and she may not be very friendly toward strangers. Don't assume she is always like this. Nursing a litter of puppies takes a lot out of female dog and instinctively makes her protective of her new babies.

When can I choose my puppy?

You may not get to choose your puppy at all. Jack Russells have small litters and some pups may already be reserved. The breeder will have a good idea of which pup would best mesh with your needs and may suggest a pup for you. You might be given a couple of pups to choose from. You may be able to choose your puppy as early as six weeks of age, but you won't be able to take him home with you until at least eight weeks of age. He still needs to be with his dam and littermates until then.

What should I look for in a puppy?

You want your pup to look and act like the Jack Russell Terrier of your dreams. And you want him to be healthy. Chances are you'll fall in love with the looks of every puppy. If you don't plan to show your dog, then you can choose whatever color pattern and coat type you find most pleasing. If you do plan to show, you will need to wait until they are older to make an informed choice—and even then, a lot of luck is involved! You'll probably also fall in love with the personalities of every puppy. You may find yourself drawn to the little hellion or the shy flower, but these extremes are best left for more experienced owners. Go for one of the calmer pups who confidently approaches you with a happy attitude.

How can I tell if the puppies are healthy?

You can get some idea simply by looking at how they are kept. Pups raised in dirty pens reflect a lack of sanitation and health care on the part of the breeder. It's probably time to leave and look for another litter. You can also do your own health check. (For more information, see Chapter 4.)

How do I do a health check?

1. Look at how the pups act. If they are listless they may be sleepy, but they may also be ill. Ask to visit again later to see if they are any livelier.

2. Look at all the pup's orifices. The ears should be fairly clean. Lots of dark debris, especially if the pup is shaking his head or scratching at his ears, could indicate ear mites. These parasites are contagious to other animals.

3. The eyes should have no gooey discharge, nor should there be red staining beneath them. A thin mucous discharge could indicate an infection or irritation. Red staining means a dog has a long-standing watery discharge. It may be not be serious, but it can be a nuisance.

4. The anus should be clean and neither red nor swollen. The latter would indicate irritation from diarrhea.

5. The penis or vulva should have only a little discharge.

6. The teeth should be fairly straight, with the upper incisors (front teeth) just barely in front of the lower ones, and the upper fangs just behind the lower ones.

   The gums should be pink. Pale gums indicate anemia, which could result from internal parasites or another illness.

7. The coat should be free of bald or red patches. Missing hair around the face, especially, could indicate demodectic mange. A few scratches are okay because puppies play roughly with one another, but keep an eye out for any sores. The coat should also be free of fleas and ticks.

8. The limbs should be strong. Puppies have growth knobs on their wrists that will disappear as they grow taller. The puppy shouldn't be limping. If your favorite is favoring one leg, ask to visit again in another day to see if he's recovered. He may simply have pulled a muscle while playing.

9. A male pup should have two tiny testicles already descended into the scrotum. Some dogs retain one or both testicles within the body. They may descend a little later, but if they don't, they should be surgically removed because they are more prone to cancer later in life. Such surgery is more difficult and expensive than a routine neutering operation.

What do I need to have on hand before I bring home my Jack Russell ?

You should have a crate, food and water bowls, chew toys, dog food, a leash and a collar and puppy-sized treats for training.

Are there any other preparations I need to make?

You need to dog-proof your house and yard. Jack Russell puppies get into everything, and some things could be deadly to them. Move all poisons, fertilizers, cleaners, automotive supplies and anything a dog could possibly swallow out of his reach. Antifreeze is a particularly deadly hazard that dogs love to drink. Even eating a penny can be deadly, because its zinc content poisons the dog as it dissolves in the stomach. Remember that Jack Russells eat things no normal-thinking dog would try. A couple of Jacks once ate a 10-pound bag of onions. Their owner found out the hard way that onions can be deadly to dogs because they destroy red blood cells. Only intensive veterinary treatment saved their lives.

Besides things they shouldn't eat, what other dangers should I protect my dog from?

Jack Russell Terrier pups are wild! They can get carried away and jump off places they shouldn't. Make sure your dog can't jump off a deck or fall down stairs. Also make sure he can't pull something over on himself or run into a clear pane of glass. In the yard, make sure your fence is absolutely escape proof. Check for tree limbs that could fall on him. If you live in an area where predators like coyotes and hawks can get into your yard, remember that a tiny Jack pup might be looked upon as prey until he grows up. All other dangers combined don't equal the biggest danger to Jack Russell longevity: getting loose and being hit by a car. Everyone in the family must be coached on how to close doors and gates securely. Screen doors can be an extra measure of security.

I can't wait for everyone to meet my new dog! Any advice?

Wait until he's settled in and gets to know you first. He's already confused and probably overwhelmed. Take it slow and let him explore his new home and meet his new family for a few days before introducing him to strangers.

What about meeting my other dog?

This depends on your other dog. It's best to let the dogs get acquainted away from your home, so your older dog doesn't feel like the new guy is invading his territory. Bring some treats and distract your older dog with them, so he comes to associate treats with the new dog. If your puppy is up to it, let both of them walk a bit on leashes near each other. Then walk home together and into the house. Don't let your older dog play too roughly with him, but do make sure he doesn't get jealous of him. This is the time to treat your first dog like a king.

What about meeting my cat?

If your Jack Russell Terrier is a pup, he's probably more likely to get hurt than your cat is. Protect him from your cat's claws. Whatever the age of your new Jack Russell, don't let him harass or chase the cat. Make sure the cat has a perch to escape to. Keep the cat or dog in a crate so the two of them can sniff each other safely and leisurely. Keep in mind that when your Jack Russell grows up, he will probably consider your cat prey and may try to hunt or harass the cat. Make sure your cat has a safe place to go, and never leave the two alone unsupervised.

What about my pet rodent?

Although some Jacks get to be friends with rabbits and even rats, these are the exception rather than the rule. More than likely, your Jack Russell will consider your rabbit or rat prey and try to hurt it. Protect these animals from your dog.

10

What About Registering My Jack Russell Terrier?

What is the cost of a Jack Russell Terrier? • Why do the prices breeders charge vary so much? • What is a pet price? • Why won't a breeder sell me a show-quality puppy if I am willing to pay for it? • Is it acceptable to haggle on the price of a puppy with a breeder? • What are other costs involved with owning a Jack Russell Terrier? • What does it mean when a Jack Russell Terrier has papers? • What other registration organizations recognize the Jack Russell Terrier? • My breeder wants to sell me a dog with Limited Registration. What is this? • My breeder wants me to sign a spay/neuter contract. What is this? • What is the benefit of having a Jack Russell who is registered with the AKC or UKC? • What if my dog looks like a Jack Russell Terrier but doesn't have papers? • How do I keep my Jack Russell Terrier from getting lost or stolen? • What is a microchip? • Why would I have my dog tattooed? • What else can I do to protect my Jack Russell from being lost or stolen?

What is the cost of a Jack Russell Terrier?

If you buy from a breeder, a Jack Russell Terrier pet puppy will cost you anywhere from $350 to $600. To some people, this seems like a lot to pay for a little dog. Remember, though, that when you are paying this price, you are basically compensating the breeder for a lot of expenses that he or she has had to incur to bring your puppy into the world. This includes the stud fee that the breeder had to pay to the owner of the male dog for use of his breeding services, as well as possible artificial insemination expense or shipping of the female dog to the male dog's owner for breeding. Other costs the breeder has paid include health certifications of the dam, veterinary care for the pregnant mother dog, vet care for the resulting puppies (examinations and inoculations) and possibly hand feeding, if this was needed because the mother dog became ill or rejected the puppies. Not to mention the amount of time the breeder put into finding the right male dog and raising the puppies until they were ready to go to their new homes. Good breeders also provide a guarantee for their puppies.

If you opt to buy a Jack Russell from a pet shop—not something dog experts recommend—you can expect to pay more than if you bought a puppy from a breeder. A pet shop Jack Russell can cost you $1,000 and upwards. This is ironic since dogs from breeders are almost always better socialized and of higher quality than dogs purchased from pet shops.

Why does it cost so much more to buy a Jack Russell from a pet shop than from a breeder?

Pet shop owners are running businesses that require they make a profit. Most pet shop owners try to turn a large profit when they sell a puppy and consider puppies to be high-ticket items in the store. To obtain the puppy in order to sell it to customers, the pet shop owner must pay a standard price for the dog from a supplier called a puppy mill. In most cases, the pet store owner then turns around and sells that same puppy to the consumer for a 100 percent mark-up or more.

Responsible breeders, on the other hand, are not breeding Jack Russell Terriers for profit. They breed dogs as a hobby with the goal of producing good-quality Jack Russells to help improve the breed—not to make money. Their puppy prices reflect their attempt to recoup the costs of breeding a dog and raising the puppies. They are not looking to make a profit and in fact are losing money in most cases.

Why do the prices breeders charge vary so much?

The price you will pay for a Jack Russell will depend on a few different factors. The first is where you live. Jack Russells, just like everything else, are cheaper in some areas of the country than in others simply because of supply and demand. The price depends on how many Jack Russell breeders are active in a certain area. If Jack Russells are popular in your area and several breeders abound, the puppies may cost less because there are more of them available. If you live in an area where Jack Russells are scarce, the pups will cost more because they are harder to come by.

Another factor is the type of Jack Russell you are buying. Serious fanciers often charge more for their puppies than do people who are breeding just for the sake of breeding, with no actual purpose to it other than to create more Jack Russells. A show breeder may charge more than others, even if the pup is not destined to be a show dog. For example, a farmer who has a litter of Jack Russell puppies available may charge less for one of his or her puppies than a show breeder typically will.

Will it cost a lot less to adopt a Jack Russell from a rescue group than to buy a puppy?

Yes. Most Jack Russell rescue groups charge an adoption fee to help them offset the costs of caring for homeless Jack Russells, but this fee is often less than what you would pay to a breeder and certainly to a pet shop. You also benefit because the dog may already be house-trained and obedience trained, which will save you money and time in the long run.

What is a pet price?

Jack Russell breeders who breed dogs for show sell puppies for show and for pets. The puppies who are sold as pets are sold at a pet price, which is considerably less than those sold as show dogs. Show dogs are much harder to come by than pet-quality puppies and so command a lot more than puppies sold as pets. Puppies considered show quality are the ones who will be priced the highest in a litter.

Why won't a breeder sell me a show-quality puppy if I am willing to pay for it?

For several reasons. First, show breeders aren't in the dog show game for the money. They breed dogs in the hopes of showing those dogs and earning a name for their kennel and for the betterment of the Jack Russell breed. Since puppies born with the kind of look needed to be show dogs are few and far between, a breeder would not be likely to place such a puppy with someone who would not show the dog. Instead the breeder would keep the dog and show the dog him- or herself or sell the dog to someone he or she knows will put the dog into competition.

Another reason a breeder may not sell you a show puppy is because the breeder may want to keep the puppy for himself- or herself, so the dog can become part of his or her breeding program. In fact, the reason most show breeders breed a litter in the first place is hopefully to get at least one show puppy from the litter who the breeder can keep for the future of the breeding program.

What if I promise to show the puppy when it grows up?

The breeder will want to see evidence that you are serious about showing dogs before selling you a show-quality Jack Russell puppy. If a breeder is reluctant to sell you a show dog, you could offer to co-own the puppy. In this situation, the puppy will live with you but will stay with the breeder when it's time for a dog show. The breeder will take the Jack to dog shows, usually on the weekends, show the dog and then return the dog to you when the last day of the show is over. If your dog turns out to be a very successful dog in the show ring, the breeder may want to campaign the dog, meaning that the breeder will take the dog out on the road frequently. The breeder may show the dog him- or herself or else turn the dog over to a professional handler for this.

Keep in mind that if you decide to co-own a show dog with a breeder, you will likely spend a good number of days without your dog at your side. Your Jack Russell will be off at shows instead of keeping you company. And if your Jack Russell is a female, your breeder co-owner will probably want to breed her for a litter of puppies. Your dog will go to live with the breeder while she is raising her litter, and you won't see much of her then, either.

Is it acceptable to haggle on the price of a puppy with a breeder?

This is not a good idea. Breeders want to know that their puppies are going to good homes where they will be loved and cared for. If a prospective owner starts debating the price of the dog as if the dog was a used car, the breeder will get the impression that you are more concerned about money than you are about the kind of dog you are getting. Responsible breeders work hard to produce sound, healthy puppies who have been well socialized. The breeder makes a commitment to that dog for the rest of the dog's life, agreeing to take the dog back if you are ever unable to keep it. From the breeder's perspective, the sale and purchase of a puppy is not about money. It's about love and companionship.

Then why don't breeders just give their puppies away?

It has been shown over and over again that when people pay money for something—even something as precious as a puppy—they give that thing more value. By selling puppies instead of giving them away, breeders are helping ensure that the puppies they produce are considered valuable and worth caring for.

Another reason breeders sell puppies instead of giving them away is that it costs the breeder considerable money to breed the female, to care for her before and after her pregnancy and to care for the puppies once they are born. The money you pay for a Jack Russell puppy helps the breeder recoup the cost of all that care, and continue his or her breeding program in the future.

What are other costs involved with owning a Jack Russell Terrier?

Aside from purchase price or adoption fee, you will also need to spend money having your Jack Russell spayed or neutered. This can cost you anywhere from $80 to $250, depending on whether your Jack Russell is a male or female and the cost of veterinary care where you live.

You'll also need to pay to have your Jack Russell inoculated several times as a puppy and once a year thereafter. Discuss vaccination protocol with your veterinarian because some are now changing their program. An annual veterinary exam is in order to keep your Jack Russell healthy, along with the purchase of heartworm preventative and flea and tick control products to prevent infestation by these pets. Should your Jack Russell become sick or injured, you will have additional veterinary bills that could actually run into thousands of dollars, depending on the problem.

Other costs include dog food, and supplies like a crate, water and food bowls, collar, leash and toys. Obedience classes are another expense, and will probably cost you anywhere from $50 to $100 for an eight-week course.

You will need to register your Jack Russell with the city or county where you live. Known as a dog license, this registration will cost you anywhere from $10 to $25 if your Jack Russell is spayed or neutered. Unspayed and unneutered dogs cost considerably more to register, depending on your locale

Are there any hidden costs?

If you're buying from a distance, expect to pay shipping costs. Airline shipping for a puppy may cost a hundred dollars or more, and you'll have to buy a shipping kennel. You'll pay a small fee to register your dog with the AKC, UKC or JRTCA. After these, you'll pay normal expenses entailed in owning any dog. That includes veterinary expenses, which will probably run a couple of hundred dollars a year, food (another couple of hundred dollars), toys (Jack Russells need an endless supply), a crate, bowls, collars, leashes and licensing. You'll also probably spend money on training classes, and possibly boarding. And unless you're very lucky, expect to spend some money replacing or repairing some of your furnishings and perhaps your fence. Some Jack Russell Terrier owners have spent even more money repairing their car upholstery when they left the dog loose in the car while they ran into the store—another reason not to leave a dog alone in a car!

What does it mean when a Jack Russell Terrier has papers?

This term refers to the dog's registration papers. When a dog is registered, the registering body sends the owner a form that indicates the dog has been registered with that organization.

In order for a Jack Russell Terrier to be registered, the dog must have proof of its purebred parentage. In other words, the person who registered the dog has to know who the mother and father are, and those dogs have to be registered with that organization or a club recognized by that organization in order for the puppy to be registered. Registration with the organization confirms that the puppy's parents are registered purebreds, and so is the puppy.

When a young puppy is advertised as having papers, this means in many cases that the puppy's litter has been registered as a litter. Each puppy in that litter is then eligible for individual registration. This is a process the new owner usually completes after he or she takes the puppy home. Older puppies (over one year of age) or adult dogs who have papers have already been individually registered. In these situations, the new owner must apply for a transfer of ownership to put the dog's papers in his or her name.

What does AKC registration guarantee and stand for?

AKC registration only guarantees that your dog is purebred, according to AKC records. Keep in mind, though, that because your dog is purebred doesn't mean that he is healthy, of show quality or anything else. It only means that his parents were purebred and that they were registered with the American Kennel Club.

This is why it is so important that you go to a responsible breeder to purchase a puppy. The caliber of the breeder you buy from will have much more influence on the quality of your puppy than just the fact that your dog has AKC papers.

You may have heard the term "AKC papers" in reference to a Jack Russell puppy or dog for sale or adoption. This terms means that the dog has been registered with the AKC.

The job of the American Kennel Club is to maintain records on the purebred dogs that it registers. If your Jack Russell Terrier is registered with the AKC, this means your dog's lineage has been recorded by the organization and kept in the AKC's computer system. If you were to breed your dog, the AKC would keep a record of who your dog was bred to and the number of puppies in the resulting litter. When each individual puppy is registered with the AKC, they will be recorded as your dog's offspring.

If your dog wins any titles in AKC-recognized competitions, whether at a dog show, an agility event or an earthdog trial, your dog's title will be officially documented with the AKC and will become part of your dog's name.

What other registration organizations recognize the Jack Russell Terrier?

The United Kennel Club, or the UKC, also recognizes the Jack Russell Terrier. The UKC is based in Michigan and is a smaller organization than the American Kennel Club. The UKC recognizes a number of breeds that are not recognized by the American Kennel Club. In fact, the UKC recognized the Jack Russell Terrier six years before the breed was accepted by the American Kennel Club.

The Jack Russell Terrier Club of America also registers Jack Russell Terriers. The JRTCA is unusual in the dog world in that most dog breed clubs do not register dogs, but simply work with the AKC or the UKC to develop breed standards, hold breed shows and educate the public about their particular breed. The JRTCA, on the other hand, maintains a full registry for Jack Russell Terriers.

Why does the Jack Russell Terrier Club of America register Jack Russells when the AKC or UKC can do it?

The JRTCA formed in 1976 to protect the working heritage of the Jack Russell Terrier. People who were concerned that the growing popularity of

Jack Russells might result in dogs losing their working instincts decided to form a club and registry that would help maintain that instinct in the breed. This can occur when people breed the dogs for appearance rather than for working instinct. The JRTCA believes that Jack Russells with strong working instincts should be bred to keep these instincts alive in the breed.

What do I need to do to register my Jack Russell Terrier with the JRTCA?

Your Jack Russell needs to meet certain requirements before he can be JRTCA registered. First, he must be at least one year old. Unlike AKC and UKC, a Jack Russell cannot be registered with the JRTCA at birth just because he has two purebred Jack Russells for parents. The dog has to prove himself worthy before being registered.

Before you can register your Jack Russell with the JRTCA you must first join the organization and be in good standing. This means you have not violated any of the club's rules or codes of ethics. You must then present a JRTCA Veterinary Certificate, a three-to-four generation pedigree, a Stud Service Certificate and a color photos of your dog.

Is the JRTCA affiliated with the AKC or UKC?

No. The JRTCA is an independent registry for Jack Russell Terriers. In fact, the JRTCA opposes recognition of the Jack Russell by the AKC and the UKC.

My breeder wants to sell me a dog with Limited Registration. What is this?

Limited registration is an AKC designation that a breeder can mark on a puppy's registration papers to indicate that the dog should not be bred. If a dog has a Limited Registration, any puppies who come from that dog are not eligible for AKC registration.

What is the purpose of limited registration?

Limited registration gives the breeder control over the use of puppies whom he or she sells. If a breeder sells you a pet-quality puppy under the assumption that your dog will not be bred, he or she can enforce that agreement by giving the dog a Limited Registration.

What if I want to breed my Jack Russell?

A responsible breeder will not sell you a Jack Russell Terrier as a pet if you plan to breed the dog. If you want to breed Jacks, you must become involved in a Jack Russell Terrier club, agree to start showing your dog and sign a Breeder Code of Ethics before you will find a breeder who will sell you a show-quality puppy you can ultimately breed. Before you breed your Jack Russell, you will need to acquire one or more titles on the dog to ensure the dog's worthiness before allowing the dog to reproduce.

Why do I need to do all this if I just want to have a litter of puppies?

Responsible breeders and those who are involved with the sport of pure-bred dogs want to limit the number of puppies who are bred. Thousands of purebred dogs are euthanized each year in animal shelters because they do not have homes. Responsible dog people do not want puppy buyers to contribute to this problem by indiscriminately breeding their dogs when the dogs are old enough.

My breeder wants me to sign a spay/neuter contract. What is this?

A spay/neuter contract is a document that will be given to you by the breeder to verify that you plan to spay or neuter your Jack Russell puppy once the dog is old enough. You will be asked to sign this contract in exchange for purchasing a pet Jack Russell Terrier. The contract may specify that you will not be given your dog's registration papers until you show proof to the breeder that you have had your dog spayed or neutered.

Why do I need a spay/neuter contract if I already have a dog with Limited Registration?

The spay/neuter contract is another way for the breeder to help ensure that you will not breed the dog you have purchased from him or her. With Limited Registration, your dog's offspring would not be registerable with the AKC. With a spay/neuter contract, you also won't receive your dog's papers until you show proof of spaying or neutering.

The American Kennel Club version of the Jack Russell Terrier, the Parson Russell Terrier, is expected to breed true to type, and so differs from Jack Russells registered with the United Kennel Club. Those breeding Parson Russells strive to breed dogs who are uniform in appearance.

What is the benefit of having a Jack Russell who is registered with the AKC or UKC?

If your dog is registered with either one of these organizations, you and your dog can participate in any of the activities these clubs sanction, as long as the events are open to terriers. Your dog will be eligible to earn titles that will become part of his registered name.

If your dog is AKC registered, you are also eligible to register him with the organization's lost and found program. The AKC uses the dog's registration number to track you down and inform you if your dog is found.

If your Jack Russell is UKC registered, he can participate in UKC events and receive titles and awards in a variety of competitions.

A less tangible benefit to AKC and UKC registration is simply the proof that your dog is a registered purebred. Knowing for certain that your dog is a purebred Jack Russell Terrier enables you to understand your dog's breed history, temperament and genetic health situation.

What kind of AKC activities are open to terriers?

Jack Russell Terriers registered with the American Kennel Club are eligible to participate in conformation dog shows, where judges evaluate the dog's physical make up, temperament and movement. Jack Russells who accumulate 15 points in a conformation dog show are designated as champions. The title of Ch. is added to the beginning of the dog's name.

Jack Russells can also compete in obedience competitions, where dogs are judged on how well they obey predetermined obedience commands given by the handler. Dogs receive different titles depending on the level of obedience skill they accomplish in the competition ring. Not many Jack Russells are seen in obedience competition because it's hard to train Jacks to perform these precise maneuvers.

Agility is another event sanctioned by the AKC that is open to Jack Russell Terriers. Agility involves negotiating an obstacle course in a timed event, where dogs are judged for speed and accuracy. Dogs receive titles added to the end of their names that reflect the level of ability they have proven in the sport.

AKC also offers terriers the chance to participate in tracking competitions. These events require the dog to follow a scent track from the beginning of a course to the end. The handler accompanies the dog on the track. Dogs can earn tracking titles that are added to the end of their names.

All of these activities are open to all breeds of dogs, but small terriers and Dachshunds are the only dogs who can participate in AKC earthdog trials. These events test the dog's ability to locate quarry in underground tunnels. Dogs who compete in these events can earn a title that is added to the end of their names.

What kind of UKC activities are open to Jack Russells?

The UKC has similar events to the American Kennel Club. Jack Russells are eligible to compete in UKC agility, obedience and conformation showing. The UKC also has an Earth Work Hunting Program for small terriers that is similar to the AKC's earthdog trials. An event unique to UKC is Cur & Feist, a hunting activity that is open to all breeds of dogs. Weight-pulling competitions are also available to Jack Russell Terriers and other breeds of dog who weigh 15 pounds or more.

Why are some AKC and UKC activities not open to terriers?

Both organizations also sponsor events that are for specific breeds or types of dogs other than the Jack Russell Terrier. Herding competitions are for herding breeds such as Collies, Shetland Sheepdogs and Pembroke Welsh Corgis, while lure coursing events, which involve chasing a lure, are only open to certain breeds of hounds. UKC hunting retriever events and AKC field trials are designed for retrieving, pointing and spaniel breeds.

Are there any activities I can participate in if my dog is not registered with one of these organizations?

Yes. The American Kennel Club allows all breeds of dogs, registered or not, as well as mixed breeds to participate in its Canine Good Citizen program. Dogs can earn their Canine Good Citizen (CGC) title by passing a test that requires them to follow some basic obedience commands. The test also evaluates the dog's temperament to see if he can handle loud noises, separation from his owner and handling by strangers. Dogs who pass the test are awarded a CGC title in the form of a certificate from the AKC. For a small fee, you can also obtain a special CGC identification tag that your dog can wear on his collar.

What if my dog looks like a Jack Russell Terrier but doesn't have papers?

Both the AKC and UKC have provisions for Jack Russells who are clearly purebred, yet have no proof of their parentage. The AKC program is called the Indefinite Listing Privilege (ILP), and the UKC program is the Limited Privilege Listing (LP). These programs require you to send photographs of your dog to the registering organization for evaluation. If AKC or UKC officials determine that your dog is indeed a purebred Jack Russell Terrier, they will issue an ILP or LP number. This number will allow your dog to compete in AKC or UKC events, just as if he had regular papers. However, it does not permit you to breed your dog. Before a dog can receive an ILP or LP number, the dog must be spayed or neutered.

What happens if I choose not to register my Jack Russell?

You won't be able to compete in activities sanctioned by these clubs. If you do not plan to show or breed your dog or compete in canine sports, there is no reason you have to register your Jack Russell Terrier.

How much does it cost to register a dog?

The American Kennel Club currently charges $15 for an individual registration, and the UKC $28.

How do I keep my Jack Russell Terrier from getting lost or stolen?

Because Jack Russells are good at jumping, digging and escaping from yards, this is an important question. Also, in certain areas, Jacks can be at risk for being stolen because of their small size. Some criminals look for small dogs they can use for the training of fighting dogs or to sell to research laboratories. The sad fact is that one out of five dogs in the United States is lost or stolen every year.

You can do a lot to keep your Jack Russell safely in your home, starting with equipping him with proper identification in the event that he gets lost.

How do I equip him with proper ID?

Start with a collar. Purchase a buckle collar for your Jack, one that is secure and fitted snugly enough that it won't come off, but not so tight that it's uncomfortable for the dog. You can use a leather collar or a nylon collar. The type of collar you choose is a matter of personal preference.

Next, have an ID tag made that you can hang from his collar. The tag can be made from plastic or metal, and should contain vital information that someone would need to find you if they located your lost dog. Your name and phone number should be there, along with your address if possible. Your Jack Russell's name is not important. It's more important that your contact info be present rather than the dog's name.

Attach the ID tag to your dog's collar, and have him wear it at all times. You never know when he might slip out of your grasp. In fact, most dogs become lost after escaping from their backyards.

In addition to the ID tag, you can ask your veterinarian to equip your dog with a microchip or opt to have your Jack tattooed.

What is a microchip?

A microchip is a small computer chip that is inserted under the dog's skin and contains a registration number. If your Jack Russell is found and taken to an animal control facility, workers at the facility will scan the dog's body for a microchip. The dog's microchip registration number will appear on the scanner, enabling the animal control agency to locate the owner.

Once your dog is microchipped by your veterinarian, you register your dog with one of the companies that tracks microchips in pets. The animal control agency will contact the microchip tracking company, and the company will contact you to let you know your dog is being held at a shelter. You can also provide an alternate contact person to retrieve your dog in the event that you are unreachable.

Why would I have my dog tattooed?

Some dog owners opt to have their dogs tattooed for identification purposes in the event the dog is lost or stolen. This may be done in addition to having a microchip implanted and attaching an ID tag to his collar.

What else can I do to protect my Jack Russell from being lost or stolen?

Always know where your dog is. Make sure your yard is secure, and don't leave him outside unsupervised. Remember that Jack Russells are great at digging, jumping and climbing. If they get bored in the backyard by themselves, they will have no qualms about finding a way out.

If you have to leave your Jack Russell alone for a few hours, leave him securely in his crate while you are gone, in your house. This will eliminate almost all likelihood of him escaping or being stolen.

Here are some other ways to protect your dog: Never leave him alone in a parked car, do not tie him up outside a restaurant or store and don't let him run loose in the woods or in a park. Someone might come along and snatch your dog, or your Jack Russell might see a rabbit or a squirrel and disappear from your sight, never to be heard from again.

How Can I Learn More?

Jack Russell Terrier Breed Clubs

Parson Russell Terrier Association of America (PRTAA)
P.O. Box 121
Lewisville, PA 19351
www.prtaa.org

Jack Russell Terrier Club of America (JRTCA)
P.O. Box 4527
Lutherville, MD 21094-4527
(410) 561-3655
www.terrier.com

Jack Russell Rescue Clubs

Parsons Russell Terrier Association of America (PRTAA) Rescue
www.prtaa.org/rescue.html

Jack Russell Terrier Club of America (JRTCA) Rescue
www.terrier.com/rescue/rescuemenu.php3

Purebred Dog Clubs

American Kennel Club
5580 Centerview Drive
Raleigh, NC 27606-3390
(212) 696-8200
www.akc.org

United Kennel Club
100 East Kilgore Road
Kalamazoo, MI 49001-5598
(616) 343-9020
www.ukcdogs.com

Canadian Kennel Club
Commerce Park
89 Skyway Ave., Suite 100
Etobicoke, Ontario, Canada M9W 6R4
(416) 675-5511
www.ckc.ca

Canine Activity Clubs

North American Flyball Association
1400 W. Devon Avenue, #512
Chicago, IL 60660
www.flyball.org

United States Dog Agility Association, Inc.
P.O. Box 850955
Richardson, TX 75085-0955
(972) 231-9700
www.usdaa.com

North American Dog Agility Council
HCR 2, Box 277
St. Maries, ID 83861
www.nadac.com

American Kennel Club (tracking, agility, obedience, field trials, hunt tests)
Performance Events Dept.
5580 Centerview Drive
Raleigh, NC 27606
(919) 854-0199
www.akc.org

American Working Terrier Association
Candy Butterfield, President
N14330 City Highway G
Minong, WI 54859
www.dirt-dog.com

Dog Training Associations

American Dog Trainers Network
New York, NY
(212) 727-7257
www.inch.com/~dogs/

National Association of Obedience Instructors
Attn: Corresponding Secretary
PMB # 369
729 Grapevine Hwy, Suite 369
Hurst, TX 76054-2085

Association of Pet Dog Trainers
P.O. Box 385
Davis, CA 95617
(800) PET-DOGS
www.apdt.com

Animal Behavior Society
Indiana University
2611 East 10th Street, #170
Bloomington, IN 47408-2603
812-856-5541
www.animalbehavior.org

Tattoo Registries

National Dog Registry
Box 116
Woodstock, NY 12498
(800) 637-3647
www.natldogregistry.com

InfoPet
P.O. Box 716
Agoura Hills, CA 91376
(800) 858-0248

Tattoo-A-Pet
6571 S.W. 20th Court
Ft. Lauderdale, FL 33317
(800) 828-8667
www.tattoo-a-pet.com

Health Organizations

Orthopedic Foundation for Animals (OFA)
2300 E. Nifong Boulevard
Columbia, MO 65201-3856.
(573) 442-0418
www.offa.org

Canine Eye Registration Foundation (CERF)
Veterinary Medical Data Program
South Campus Courts, Building C
Purdue University
West Lafayette, IN 47907
(765) 494-8179
www.vet.purdue.edu/~yshen/cerf.html

Veterinary Pet Insurance (VPI)
4175 E. La Palma Avenue, #100
Anaheim, CA 92807-1846
(714) 996-2311
www.petinsurance.com

National Animal Poison Control Center
1717 S. Philo, Suite 36
Urbana, IL 61802
(800) 548-2423

ASPCA Animal Poison Control Center
(888) 426-4435
www.aspca.org/site/PageServer?pagename=apcc

Pet Loss Hotlines

University of California, Davis
530) 752-4200

Tufts University School of Veterinary Medicine (Massachusetts)
(508) 839-7966

Virginia-Maryland Regional College of Veterinary Medicine
(540) 231-8038

Michigan State University College of Veterinary Medicine
(517) 432-2696

Washington State University College of Veterinary Medicine
(509) 335-5704

Books

The Angell Memorial Animal Hospital Book of Wellness and Preventive Care for Dogs, Darlene Arden, McGraw-Hill/Contemporary Books, 2002.

The Complete Dog Book, 19th Edition, Revised American Kennel Club, Howell Book House, 1998.

The Dog Owner's Home Veterinary Handbook, 3rd Edition, James M. Giffin, MD, and Lisa D. Carlon, DVM, Howell Book House, 2000.

Dog Training in 10 Minutes, Carol Lea Benjamin, Howell Book House, 1997.

Earthdog Ins and Outs: Guiding Natural Instincts for Success in Earthdog Tests and Den Trials, Jo Ann Frier-Murza, OTR Publications, 1998.

Jack Russell Terrier: Courageous Companion, Catherine Romaine Brown, Howell Book House, 1999.

Index